THREE
SIMPLE
THINGS

THREE SIMPLE THINGS

Leading During Chaos

THOM SHEA

Clovercroft Publishing

Three Simple Things

©2020 by Thom Shea

Published by Clovercroft Publishing, Franklin, Tennessee

Edited by Tammy Kling

Copy Edited by Gail Fallen

Cover and Interior Design by Suzanne Lawing

Printed in the United States of America

Trade Paperback Version 978-1-950892-48-8

Hardcover Version 978-1-950892-58-7

Foreword

by Thom Shea

This book grinds out the story about my life after the SEAL teams facing a complex new world and finding three simple things. The manner in which I have chosen to tell the details are intended to resemble the times when warriors or hunters would come back home and relay their tales of victory and defeat around the bonfire with their children and family. Every warrior wants to pass on to the next generations what they have learned in some meaningful way.

Ironically, I don't think that my personal drama is of any value. Where I was born and where and how I lived are unimportant. The measurable value is what I have done that can be learned and passed on.

While I have a past, killed men in war, saw my brothers die, lost a marriage, I am not my past. No one really is their past.

I am particularly pleased that after five years of training leaders to lead during chaos that each has asked me to write about the process and methods to produce results. The training is so difficult I never considered they would be open to sharing the simple details.

For me the world has become very complex. This book makes the complex simple.

Introduction to
Three Simple Things

Look around you. We humans make our lives painfully complex. Relationships, which are fundamentally simple, now team with complexity. The boring simplicity of being physically tough and in shape drowns in a swamp of exciting complex and lazy actions. The pursuit of wealth evolved away from simple work and simple teamwork to a virtual devaluing of hard work into hacks and overindulgent actions that have no value. The simple act of learning is now mired in politics and debt. Spiritually, we are void of meaning to the point a simple prayer or meditation signifies depression and loss of soul.

There are five areas in each of your lives that demand simplicity and abhor complexity: Spiritual, Relationship, Wealth, Physical, and Intellectual. To win, you need only do three simple things in each. Success is simple, but not easy!

Three Simple Things is written in the manner of old storytelling. Real stories, told around a campfire, where people gathered to learn from the warriors and leaders of the tribe or village. The words are intended to be read as if you and I are next to each other talking frankly without political correctness. The stories are also meant to feel urgent and necessary. I ask you to integrate each chapter into your life.

My intent for you is to achieve a six-hour baseline during your day-to-day life. I have spent my adult life as a Navy SEAL, developing and honing the only five measurable areas of life as the baseline for sustained growth: physical health, structured learning, wealth creation, meaningful relationships, and spiritual connections. Over the past six years, I have trained leaders and athletes and coaches in order to produce a baseline of three simple things in their lives so that they lead teams or companies toward success. The process is rather straightforward; the various methods are definable and clear. The effort is simple, but not easy. As you learn the process and method, you will achieve measurable outcomes by just maintaining the baseline. The maintenance of the baseline is nonnegotiable.

To My Children

Three Simple Things is for you! The older I get, the more I realize the limited time I have to prepare you for life. My deepest wish is to pass on everything I have learned in my life to add some measurable value to yours. Many of my SEAL brothers did not return home from war. Many who did return are injured, many have post-traumatic stress; many have brain injuries and cannot pass on to their families the vast knowledge and experiences acquired in their lives. Read these reflections so all the combined knowledge will be useful to you. I write this as if I was sitting and talking to you with no pretenses or formality, only with urgency.

To the Readers I Have Never Met

I am a fan of the human experience of growth and have spent 50 years thriving in the chaos of war and the chaos of everyday life. We all have vast stores of experiences and knowledge we want to pass on to friends, family, and others. Thank you for your willingness to absorb my experiences and your desire to break through your own chaos to find three simple things in your own life.

If you are interested in sustained, high-level performance in the five measurable areas of your life, called pyramids, then the processes and methods I will describe are for you. If you are only interested in comfort, only excited about one pyramid, or only want to learn a short-term hack, then this is not for you. We humans have arrived at the most abundant time for wealth creation; the deepest pools of opportunity to achieve physical goals; the furthest capacity to learn; the most profound ways to relate to each other; and the clearest sense of spiritual connections in our evolution. When you are interested in tangible success, *Three Simple Things* is for you!

Any of us willing to put into practice the fundamentals of learning, practicing, and maintaining a baseline will achieve levels of performance far beyond what we now think possible. Like all great endeavors, all you need to do is commit. Commit before you know the end result. Commit without the notion that you can exit when it gets chaotic. Commit, because without commitment nothing measurable is possible. Once you are committed, then there is just "work" to do. During the process of working on the six-hour baseline, don't give up on yourself. Quitting or giving up has no place in this life. Quitting has killed more marriages, cut short more athletic endeavors, caused more business failures, and always separates each of us from divine access.

The baseline is not about balance. For some strange reason there is a movement to balance life. Balance in any sense literally means taking bits from one and putting into another or even getting rid of those bits to have balance. Time cannot be balanced, energy cannot be balanced, and life or passion cannot be balanced. The pursuit of balance always leads to the inevitable conclusion where you have to avoid one thing to have another, and at the extreme part of balance is the notion that stress is bad and needs to be avoided. The absence of stress will destroy you. Embrace stress and stop negotiating with what matters and doesn't matter. Instead I offer a nonnegotiable life!

You can live in a bubble with no gravity, with no negative stimuli, which is where the pursuit of balance will take you. In the bubble, after a short time, your body will deteriorate . . . and so will your ability to think. You will never find balance; the notion is folly and simply a sales pitch from a scared child who has quit on his or her life.

I offer a simple truth: do three simple things in the five pyramids of performance and carve out six nonnegotiable hours and activities a day as the foundation for truly living life. You will not balance time to achieve the baseline, nor will you give up one category for another.

You will literally create a baseline to think and grow. From the six-hour baseline, I have seen men and women run ultramarathons, grow their wealth by two times in a year, turn around a failing marriage, and start a new life and thrive.

For the past six years of sustaining my own six-hour baseline while training and witnessing my clients struggle through a life of not having the nonnegotiable baseline, but instead overweighting one pyramid while destroying the other four areas of life, I am very clear on the value of sharing the process and method with you. I noticed businessmen and women work a 12-hour day and produce millions while neglecting family and health. I witnessed great athletes training for 7 hours a day and produce number-one status while excluding relationships and lacking the ability to find a dollar in a bank. I have seen parents spend up to 6 hours a day shuttling kids around while giving up their own health and ambitions. Negotiating with life, always adjusting to the changes without having a nonnegotiable baseline, causes epic long-term failures. The baseline will allow you to achieve much more in each of the five pyramids.

Shocking as that may seem to you, the conditions I just described are found everywhere in our society. The new norm, as it seems, always ends badly. But everyone seems to be on this railroad leading to a cliff of destruction. And, trust me, the cliff where the train falls off going full speed was happening for every successful executive, every top athlete, and seemingly every marriage.

The executives literally worked with the thought process to build a business to make money to support their family and lifestyle. Twelve-hour workdays, as I began to notice, were killing the family because there was no family time or activity. The extreme focus on work excluded health and created a horrible eating, sleeping, and activity cycle. As I continued to notice over time what was occurring in this overweighted life paradigm, the inevitable outcomes of running the train off the cliff became predictable.

At some point in time, the leader would give up half of the income to the spouse. Divorce cuts income by half, let's not quibble. After all those hours, all those *years* of working a 12-hour day, the money would be cut in half, not to mention the exhausting process of a divorce. It was predictable. After two years of seeing all the indicators and developing a series of questions, I began to realize I could even "short the market" and bet against the companies' success simply because the boss' work-to-family life ratio was off.

The most disturbing aspect of the overworked leader became deadly clear looking at the lack of any tangible commitment to physical health. I will describe the details later; however, neglect in physical health didn't lead to going over a cliff, but it led straight into a brick wall. The 12-hour normal workday eventually kills the leader. Yes, they die or get so sick they can no longer work, or they die within two years of retiring. As it were, they were losing everything at the end. Leaving a trust for the kids seemed to be the norm because most had a trust fund set up by age 50 and knew they were sick and not doing well. The scary part is everyone was doing this. We all seemed to be in a rat race no one could avoid or we just can't get off the flywheel.

The leaders and top performers had negotiated themselves out of sustainable performance in the five pyramids. More of one pyramid is alluring. Being number one is too. Yet, without a baseline, without the rest of your life being on point, none of the accumulation of stuff is sustainable. The six-hour baseline of doing three simple nonnegotiable things in each of the five pyramids of life literally make success easier and much more sustainable. The rest of the book is stories about the detailed processes and methods to follow in order to set up and maintain a six-hour baseline.

Contents

Never Give Up!

In my time in leadership and training leaders, I've developed foundational principles to achieving sustainable performance. Like most great principles of success, my own life experiences have given me a lot of clarity about the things that matter. There are several critical principles of success; however, two core principles stand out. These are the two traits that every great leader I've observed has, and they are resilience (the ability to never give up and stay the course) and integrity and consistency, which is honoring your word.

The ability to honor your word literally is the core principle of all success. The inability to honor your word distinctly causes failure. Those who can't honor their word are inconsistent and often unreliable.

Honoring Your Word Matters

Let's talk more about this foundational principle and how it applies to your own life. What do I mean by "honoring your word"? Even though the human race is on the brink of real greatness, the "honoring your word" principle is rare. Making a promise and keeping it is very rare. Getting expressed commitment from one out of 1,000 people is stunningly rare. Often this rarity would be called persistence or even relentlessness. Those two words are mere adjectives describing a more fundamental principle. The deepest principle in success is honoring your word, which is rooted in integrity.

All leaders lead with fear or hesitation, yet they lead in spite of it.

Leading is solely about consistency, relentlessness, and asking more of yourself than you do others. Leading by honoring your word and never giving up will define everything that you say or do. Do you honor yourself, your time, and your team?

The ability to say something, then to go and do what you said you would do, will set you apart from the herd. Even in the smallest aspects of your life, when you master the principle of honoring your word, your actions will lift you up and success will happen. What if you said you would make your bed, then you actually made your bed?

What if you said you would do your homework, and you actually did your homework? What if you said you would do 100 pushups a day for 21 days, and you actually did the pushups? What if you said you would talk to one new prospect a day, then you actually talked to one a day? What if you said you would be faithful to your spouse and you actually honored your word? Imagine the level of success, peace, and performance you would achieve.

Kill Your Excuses

Those simple questions, as you can tell, shock your brain into realizing how rare a thing honoring your word is in this world. A simple truth: success is not easy. In order to honor your word, you must kill off all of your learned excuses. Trust me, excuses are all learned. The practice of killing off your excuses and your reasons for not honoring your word will be the hardest aspect of success you will find in the pages that follow. Killing off my own excuses has not only taken my lifetime but also is a daily adventure.

I have seen men ripped apart in combat get up and fight their way back to safety. I have seen marriages that could never hope to continue due to poor choices reset and begin anew. I have witnessed runners completely fall apart and break down emotionally and physically only to rally and finish 100-mile ultramarathons. All done by killing off their excuses and reasons and getting back to the foundational principle of success, which has always been to honor your word.

On the other hand, I've seen those with the most basic and minimal obstacles in life crumble because they excused themselves from doing the simple things. All across the world you can see examples of this, whether it's in health or relationships or in their business lives. Taking days off being on point in health; excusing ourselves from the simple prospect of reading with our kids or even playing their video games with them; and even missing work opportunities because we do not feel like it. How do you learn to kill your excuses on a daily basis? The solution is simple.

Be the person you said you would be, no matter the conditions.

In each of the following chapters is a story and a process with step-by-step methods to build the foundation and structure for success. The experience of turning around the "wayward vessel" of my own life by recognizing my excuses, then being bold enough to share the facts, remains the most difficult story I wish to convey. The brutal challenge to be a part of other men and women sharing their "failure to success" processes is the second most difficult aspect of forming the stories within the following chapters. As we work through both the writing and the digesting of the stories together, I encourage you to be bold enough to read and to apply the processes and methods in your day-to-day life.

Nothing Left to Lose

My personal foundational story is the American story. Only in America can you have the freedom and safety to completely fail and build from the ashes of that experience. Our founding fathers came here to rebuild; our families now rebuild constantly. In fact, we are the rebuild nation. We are not a nation of laws. We are a republic of states, built on the notion that people can rebuild themselves and earn their lives.

I grew up during the '70s and '80s. A time with no restrictions, it seemed. A time when you could carry a gun in your truck so you could hunt after school to put meat on the table, a time when you could fistfight at school and take your punishment. And a time when parents told their kids they could do anything they wanted as long as they earned it themselves.

That attitude, that grace of parenting, and that occasional bloody nose encouraged me to earn a spot at the United States Military Academy. But that is not the story. That story, had I succeeded, would be boring or just an off-the-cuff remark about an elite kid. I am common and not elite at all.

The real story that matters is that I failed out my junior year. The crushing of the soul that happens to so many of our friends and neighbors around us didn't happen to someone else, and it fractured me. For me, I was broken, I had proven to myself that I was not capable, and worse it seemed that society agreed with my assertion.

Flying home having failed was surreal. So real I can recall every smell and sound and how I felt. I was not numb as some recall their bottomless pits after failure. I was just overwhelmed with senses and had no direction. That complete loss of direction, that feeling of nothingness, lasted a long time.

Oddly, my parents were not disturbed by the failure. They both were, however, scared I would never recover. Like all great parents of that time who came from nothing, they merely provided a safe place to land. They didn't put me down; they didn't talk down to me at all. I am grateful for their strength. That strength today remains rare, indeed.

Nonetheless, the total nightmare of not knowing who I was anymore coupled with the sensation that I could never achieve a goal anymore was startling. As a young man I felt depressed and exhausted, which are still two reactions I loathe. For an old man now looking back, the sense was that I had nothing left to lose. I do not think many kids have parents who afford them the profound grace of rebuilding from loss.

During those first dangerous months with no footing, with no future, with no desire to do anything in particular, my friends fell away . . . and so did my options. As with all bouts of depression and loss, I gained weight, grew long hair, and even contemplated getting my ear pierced. Times of not knowing cause the demons to surface, that fact is very clear. The old saying "misery loves company" is true. Humans seek out people and actions that make them feel connected. When you are lost, you find others who are too.

After the "forever depressed" period of three months, my father and I had the inevitable sit down to discuss my options. The days leading up to the sit down, he merely asked me to come up with three options of jobs, or options I wanted to pursue. He offered three options: find what gives you passion, find a job, or find a college that will accept you. Yet he prefaced my search with a point of clarity: "After our sit down, you will pick one and go do it immediately. Or you will have to get a job here in town and begin to pay rent."

Brilliant tactic of a wise old man, to be sure! Dad knew I could not bear the insult of getting a job washing windows in my hometown. And to pay rent at home would mentally cripple me. The tactic worked and brought the much-needed clarity I required to carve a new path into my future.

I am sharing this story because only in America can you go after something that excites you, even though you have failed. Getting a job to make rent did not move me. I am glad I didn't pick that choice. Going back to college was about as appealing as sticking a hot poker in my eye. In fact, I was scared to share what excited me with my dad or anyone. Even to this day, the sharing of what excites me always feels fragile. When I sat there trying to share with Dad, the sharing seemed as fragile as a moth's wings. I shared because I had nothing left to lose.

"Well, I am going to Minnesota to work at a fishing outfitter, because I long to be outside and want to see if that lifestyle is possible!" I said. "I leave next Monday."

While I sat there holding the fragile future that excited me, he merely said, "Good choice. Take nothing from your past, don't look back, and never give up."

If you have ever started over, then you know what it is like to take the first step. The catharsis of leaving everything excites like no other. The freeing feeling is like a narcotic. The drive up to the outfitters was more exciting than going to West Point. In my thoughts, outdoor work represented who I was, not something I had to do or something I had to pass through. The job only paid $1,000 per month with room and food included. The job only lasted from April to October, but that had no bearing. I felt free and it felt like me.

Those six months of freedom closed out my thinking that I was a wholesale failure and encouraged me to ask and answer one simple question:

If there was nothing left to lose, what would I spend my life doing?

As you read my answer, a quick warning. My answer is mine, and not something I recommend to anyone. Never seek out someone else's life because it seems cool or exciting or better than yours. Find your own life and pursue it until the day you slide into the grave sideways, laughing.

When all my options were laid on the table like a deck of cards, I sifted through the face cards and quickly realized a high-end, luxury life did not appeal to me. I surely did not want normal, which represented the rest of the playing cards. I really, really was drawn to the joker cards. My two joker cards were Navy SEAL or sniper. Most great goals make no sense to other people, and these two choices really got the same response as having a joker in your hand. It just didn't fit in or make sense how to play these cards. As I kept shuffling the deck and always coming back to SEAL and sniper, I knew what I was going to do. The only issue was, I didn't know how to swim.

That morning I went and signed up for SEAL training. I had nothing to lose. I definitely didn't know how to swim. But I did know that without committing and giving myself no way out, I would be doomed to end up back at home having failed once again.

The drive away from signing up was again like driving up to Minnesota. I felt free, excited, and scared. The intoxicating reality of pushing into something with no return had once again gripped me. The act represented what I now call "honoring your word." You must find this in your life to truly live. You must bet everything on your word and sign a document in front of someone else who will hold you to it. True power!

If I ended my story there, at *Wow, sign up for the SEAL training and all will work out*, the story would not be of any value. Many encouraging stories don't really represent the reality of the life we all live. The rest of my story is the real struggle and the real power of honoring your word and never giving up.

Class 195

Clearly, learning to swim and passing the entrance test to Basic Underwater Demolition/ SEAL (BUD/S) training happened. I hired a swim coach and swam every day until I passed the test. Simple, but not easy! The method works every time.

I arrived to start class 195 with 87 other crazy dudes. Nothing abnormal happened. We did ungodly amounts of push-ups and flutter kicks and pull-ups. The instructors really seemed not to care if we died or lived, so we ran until someone would puke or quit or break something. We swam until someone would puke or nearly drown or quit. This seemed to get worse every single day. People were quitting so often, and for some reason, it really felt lonely. My friends of the day before would quit and be out of the room before the end of the day. I do not recall feeling brave or tough. I felt normal. I don't know why I felt normal. I really enjoyed the straightforward brutality of the instructors and the training.

Everything seemed to be going great until "Hell Week." Hell Week is the six-days-without-sleep part of training that weeds out all the quitters who don't have what it takes to thrive in chaos. Surf torture was a non-event for me because it was just cold and seemed to make everyone else panic. I loved to see people panic and quit. And here is the real truth about tough times: all the most pristine athletes panic and quit during surf torture.

After surf torture we paddled the boats down to the rocks in front of the Hotel del Coronado. Everything seemed to be going really well. I felt great. I was warm again. Albeit I was now the tallest guy in my boat, which meant when we carried the boat on our heads, my neck would be destroyed, but I didn't care. All we had to do was successfully land our boat on the rocks during an eight-foot swell and get our boat and crew over to the beach. The landing would be as easy as eating a bowl of ice cream melting on a hot day. I recall seeing the rocks and our boat landing well. I was the first guy out to grab the bowline and secure my footing in the rocks to keep the boat from going back out during the ebb. I have to admit I did keep the boat from going out. But the breaker behind it came in and lifted the boat up and smashed my head between it and the rocks. I don't recall that part. It was explained to me some time later over a beer.

When I came to my senses, I was laying in the SEAL training medical room. My head was bloody, and I recall cussing, then asking what had happened. Two instructors approached, one carrying the bell, the other brandishing paperwork. The one with paperwork said, "Okay, ring the bell so we can get back to training. You are done." The other pushed the bell in front of me.

I cussed again, saying, "No!"

"Don't argue with me, you quit because you got injured! Getting injured is quitting. Stop wasting my time and ring the bell three times and go back home to your parents and tell them how you got injured. We don't want quitters or people who get injured and leave their team," he said rather convincingly.

I said no again.

They both turned and walked away.

That night, alone in my room, the reality of failure gripped me again. Not knowing my fate, not knowing what was next, stared me right in the face again. However, I did not seem lost. The thought did occur they had already out processed me, and when I checked in at 8:00 a.m., my orders to be "haze gray and underway" completed and signed. I wasn't going to quit. I wasn't going to ring that bell. I didn't care if the admiral ordered me to.

I got up and put on my uniform and walked that long walk to the medical department. Just like before on the plane ride home from

West Point, my senses were heightened, albeit my head hurt quite a bit more than I was willing to admit. Quitting was not my option. My resolve was to simply ask for another opportunity to make it through training. The primary thoughts of leaving training and my dream were far scarier than the secondary thought of going home as a quitter or a failure.

While I sat in medical awaiting my fate that I had by blunder, left in the hands of someone else because I got injured, the quitters who had actually rung the bell three times formed around me. As a whole, none of them were looking me in the eyes. I find that odd to recall after all these years. One asked me what had happened, and with my normal, snappy retort I said, "I got knocked out on rock portage."

He said, "Yeah I saw that and said, 'enough,' after they pulled you away." His response didn't seem to register with my brain. I looked away, shaking my head. I feel sorry for him now, because I know he will surely deal with being a quitter every day for the rest of his life.

After some time, the chief of the training phase came out and looked at me and said, "Follow me!" Chief Mahrer scared me because he was matter of fact and always seemed to be holding all the cards. We went into the first phase office, and he made me stand in front of the bell. Lord, that seemed like an eternity, waiting and waiting and waiting.

"Shea, get in here," he said. In the office were Mahrer and another instructor. Mahrer spoke the words I will remember until I die. "Shea, I want to tell you a truth: there is no difference between getting injured and quitting in combat. If you quit, you leave the team one man short. If you get injured, you do the same thing. We are here to get rid of those two types of people. Do you understand that?"

I couldn't think of a response that made sense, so I simply said, "I didn't quit!"

They both looked at me. "Okay," Mahrer finally said, "you have another chance, but you have to start over at the beginning of first phase."

For a moment the feeling of weightlessness happened. Maybe I was about to faint. The only words I could say were "I won't quit, chief."

He looked up emotionless as ever and said, "We shall see. The second time is much harder. Few make it through the second chance."

Class 196

Mahrer was correct. The next class was distinctly harder. From my point of view, the instructors seemed to loathe this class leader for some reason unbeknownst to the students. The first morning inspection went badly, I mean *really* badly. My room didn't even get inspected. We went to the surf zone and got punished for something none of us seemed to be aware of. The order was given to bear crawl down to the obstacle course and stand by in the push-up position.

On any given day the obstacle course is hard to pass, even harder if you are wet and sandy and already tired. The course was about three quarters of a mile through the sand from where we started crawling toward the starting line. Along the way one person just stood up and walked over to the bell and rang it three times. The rest of us pushed on. By the time we all arrived at the starting line, it was an hour later.

I could not even stay in the push-up position without my arms collapsing. I knew the obstacle course was all upper body strength. For the first time in my life, I was facing something I knew I couldn't do. It was daunting.

The first five students were on the course, and my name was called. Upon standing, I felt exhausted. The first obstacle was like trying to pick up an elephant with noodles. Once over the low wall, I heard the siren go off, signifying an injury. With that I stopped and took a knee as the class leader took a headcount and the instructors dealt with the injured student. The brief rest was needed. Then the reality of the injury took shape. A student had fallen off the "Slide for Life" and broken his back upon hitting the ground. Mahrer was right.

Mahrer was walking around the students and saw me and walked straight over to where I was kneeling. "If you don't do things in life correctly the first time, it always takes twice as long and is twice as hard to do it right the second time." With that, he walked away.

No truer words have ever been said regarding life's big challenges. Now I was faced with a course that already had an 8 percent attrition rate when you try the first time. I wondered what the attrition rate was the second time as the instructors yelled to start again.

The rest of the class 196 first phase leading up to Hell Week was just like this every day: twice as hard, mentally brutal, physically overwhelming. Hell Week started with a blur, but the weather was warm and so was the water. On Tuesday we were back at the obstacle course to attempt to take the entire boat and crew up and over each obstacle. We had had no sleep at all since Saturday night. The majority of the quitters had exited, and we were down to 36 students from 72. I personally felt strong, so I went up the obstacle first to help get the boat over. My arm was stabilizing the boat as the rest of the boat crew climbed up. One of my buddies lost his grip and fell into the boat. The sudden jarring of the boat caused my shoulder to separate and the pain was rather interesting. I gritted my teeth as my swim buddies looked at me. We all knew what had happened, but if an instructor noticed it, I would be out again. We all stayed quiet and continued on.

I knew if I made it to Wednesday night at midnight, I would be rolled forward and not back to first day. At least that was how I was processing the shoulder being out of its socket and the purple color of my hand. I kept it hidden until after dinner on Tuesday night. The after-dinner festivities of Hell Week are without a doubt the most painful. Lifting the boat up over our heads and keeping it up there is hard even if you are strong. I was not strong at this point.

Mahrer, in his ever-calm demeanor, noticed the color in my hand and the fact my arm was no longer up over my head pushing up on the boat. "Shea, get your hand up on that boat and help your team," he actually whispered. "You have five seconds, or you are kicked out of training for refusal to train."

The sudden feeling of falling apart once again gripped me. "Chief, I can do this with one arm. I can hold my weight," I said.

"5, 4, 3, 2, 1," he counted. "Okay, step out, you are done."

The rest of the night was again a blur, and I went to the hospital. The doctors used traction and some muscle relaxants to pop my shoulder back into place, admittedly more painful than the separation. And I sat in the bed again, not knowing my fate. I had tried so hard. I had done all that I possibly could do. The longer I sat, the lower I felt. My thoughts were centered around "is this all worth it?" Had I just set myself up to fail at something impossible so that the failing would be believable?

I always think it's funny how we question ourselves when things go south. How we look at our struggles and try to find a way out of them instead of a way through them. There are always 1,000 ways to exit every problem: a thousand ways to quit.

The way forward was gray and unclear and profoundly disturbing. No one ever gets a third try, ever. I didn't even want to try it again. My shoulder would not recover in three weeks, which was when the next class would be starting. I sat there.

After two days, Mahrer showed up at the hospital in uniform this time. He didn't have a bell, which was the first point I noticed. He didn't have any paperwork, which was striking. Mahrer came in directly without knocking. "How is the shoulder?" he asked, and I could tell he didn't really care.

"They put it back in" is all I could muster to say.

"Shea, you get two weeks' vacation. When you return you go directly to the rehab clinic! You will miss class 197 and go directly to class 198. Do you have any questions?" He dropped the grenade in my lap knowing I would not have any.

"When you leave the hospital, check in to first phase. They have your leave paperwork. Go somewhere and get your mind right and come back," he said in his matter-of-fact nature. Then he said something again that rings as true today as it did then. "Don't go home to your parents or girlfriend or old friends. They will talk you out of coming back." With that, he turned and walked away.

My job in the Navy up to this point was as a corpsman. With the little training I had received, I knew the recovery for a dislocated shoulder was supposed to be more than six weeks. As a matter of fact, you weren't supposed to even start working out hard for six weeks. The cards were stacked against me. As I looked down at my stupid arm and reached over and touched my shoulder, which immediately produced a sharp pain, I again felt the feeling of falling. This time I was falling and could not see the bottom. That sensation is brutal to feel, even though, lately, that was the feeling I seemed to be having the most. Failing and falling, getting back up, being enthused, and repeating the cycle seemed to be my life. However, this episode of falling didn't produce the enthusiasm. I dreaded having to start over again. My body and my mind were toast. I had no respect for myself anymore. I sat there falling and spinning.

I even recall thinking, "Man I am tough, but I wonder if this is what caused people to commit suicide." Not knowing what my future would be. Clearly seeing no way to recover my shoulder. The feeling made me angry and actually angry with other people.

Six weeks later I passed the entrance test with 105 pushups and 18 pull-ups. Off to the races, once again! Off to the last chance I would have to become a SEAL. Hell Week came without incident. Surf torture was a nonevent. The boat crew obstacle course appeared and disappeared in my mind. The freezing cold of the mud flats became the new sensation of how cold and miserable one could become. Two students left with flesh eating bacteria during that trial. Everything seemed normal, except I couldn't stop coughing. By Wednesday night I was coughing up blood with each cough. As we processed through the medical screen, I was again pulled out. Pulled out to face Mahrer once again.

My walk to the first phase office in the dark was different. I cried because I realized sometimes not quitting wasn't enough. I cried because I had let Mahrer down once again. Rounding the corner, I saw the bell in front of the office. If I rang it this would all end, and the strain would be over. I could go home and not face this pain and feeling of falling. I could just hit bottom and be done with it. With each step it seemed like the best choice. The closer I got to the bell, the stronger the pull to ring became. Still, when I stood there in front of it, seeing all those helmets, all those people who had tried and quit, I couldn't do it.

Mahrer appeared in the door to the office, not seeming so intimidating as before. "Quit if you want. We aren't going to kick you out. None of us would have gone through three first phases. Now, we don't know anyone to do four. I personally think you get sick or injured as a way out. You have to defeat that demon before it kills you. I don't care if you have pneumonia or flesh-eating bacteria in your lungs. Class 199 starts Monday. You don't have to do the class up test. So show up or quit. The choice is yours," he said, actually smiling this time.

By the way, no one recovers from pneumonia in five days. And, truth be told, I certainly didn't recover. I showed up Monday with a fever and barely passed the timed run. For the next several weeks, I just barely passed everything. I was beaten like everyone else who failed or didn't improve upon previous times. Each night I stopped caring about it all. I made it into Hell Week once again . . . not caring, not sure why I was doing it, and not willing to quit.

On Wednesday night they took me to the hospital with all five lobes 50 percent infiltrated with fluid. They didn't need to tell me, I knew. I knew it was over. After a week in the hospital, and with no instructor coming to check on me, I knew it all was over. When I reported to the first phase office, they had orders for me to a new command and no one even mentioned training or anything. They had all moved on and I was insignificant to their day-to-day lives.

Completing Hell Week solidified my firm stance on the principle of "honor your word." I realized in that exact moment of walking away, as you must also realize, that this is the point in life where you either keep on honoring your word or you just quit. Once again, the world did not give me what I wanted in the timeline I had wanted it. Once again, things did not work out the way my brain had perceived events should have. Being cast out again, having to literally lie there in the puddle of mud I had created again, trying to figure out who I was and where I was going, will always be the roughest time in my life. The moment of clarity came when I realized I could actually honor my word and start over.

No one should avoid feeling the gravity of failing or the weight of loss. Both my experience then, and in training leaders now, makes me realize the importance of this transition point. At this transition point, we all have three choices.

The first choice is made by a small group of people for various, truly believable reasons. They decide to simply quit on themselves, go home (and hope and pray), and leave a goal-driven life behind. The gravity felt is too heavy to experience and quitting seems to be the only way out. An observable truth is when this path is chosen as a coping mechanism to deal with failure, it will forever be a means of dealing with every loss or failure. The undeniable fact remains: "How you do one thing, is how you do everything."

The second choice to be made, the one which most people make, seems the most obvious and least risky. I call it the backup plan. The numerous people who actually pick the backup plan clearly pushes the prevalence as you can find hundreds of books on backup plans and mitigating risk. Millions of dollars can be made mitigating risk of a bad decision and having solid backup plans that keep people from feeling the gravity of failure and loss.

I surely saw both options during my time of feeling the weight of loss once again. Going home to the safety of my father and mother and a small town was rather enticing. Quitting is the sailor's siren song. Leaving the storm for the perceived safety of a cove is really hard to push away. But sailors and boats are meant to be at sea. I had chosen to be a SEAL; that was my sea.

The backup plan principle will seem to take the weight of loss from you. In hindsight, the backup plan model itself causes loss. The time wasted while you are engaged in securing the backup plan robs the primary plan of any potential to succeed. Most people who have a backup plan will eventually move to it, because the reality of a primary plan is simply that primary plans never work out the first time. I find it tragic to push two plans and always move to the backup plan when the primary plan falters the first time. Maybe I would have taken the backup plan had I had one. I did not have plan B; I had no way out, thank God!

What occurred to me during those months after being kicked out of BUD/S training was the gravity of giving very little measurable value to my word, my original word. I had to ask myself what I had actually lost. I had lost nothing because I didn't have anything. I had to ask myself what I had failed at doing. I had not failed; I had been kicked out. The longer I let myself feel the weight and not immediately move to plan B or to quit, the clearer my situation became.

If I quit now, I was only quitting on the value of my word. I would be dishonoring my ability to say I was going to do something, anything, and then go and do it, no matter what.

Had I selected something else, I would also have lost all the value of my word holding any power in the world. The longer I carried that weight of loss, the more I began to see the power of honoring your word. I saw that to honor my word meant I had to stay committed. I had to finally admit I had quit on myself at West Point. I had to admit I did let the circumstances dictate the outcome instead of honoring my word and pushing through the circumstances.

Two months after being kicked out of BUD/S training, I committed all of myself to honoring my word to become a SEAL. At that exact moment in time, all the perceived weight, all the drama and depression, all the lack of direction ceased. I got back on point with my job. I had clear direction and wrote out a special request to present to my admiral with exactly what I wanted. I saw in his office for my entire lunch period, every single day, for six months. Each day, he repeated the same answer: No. I was written up. I was punished by my chain of command but I would not give up; for me, there was no other way. The last time I submitted it, the admiral finally relented and signed it despite all the no's he had given up to that day.

Class 207

We started with 111 students. We graduated 11 of those students. At the end of Hell Week, Mahrer spoke to the class. We were beaten, tired, and didn't care about circumstances, but we would have kept going had they asked us to. He said these 13 words: "You did what you said you would do! Now you are of value!"

The Process and Method to Honor Your Word

Stories from real people drive the point home when dealing with principles of success. The topics and chapters that follow incorporate the wise old learning method: define the topic, tell a real-life story, and show the detailed process to produce your own results using the same method. My real intent is that when I die, all that I have learned and overcome will not be lost in my passing. Human life must always be shared in its raw, visceral form so those who come after don't waste their lives treading water, making the exact same mistakes we did.

The American military as a whole learned the value of passing on both the good or bad, in stories and real experiences. Listen and watch the senior leaders, learn skills that have adapted over the past 200 plus years, and evolve. If their examples were not valuable, we would be riding horses and shooting muzzle loaders and lining up in front of our enemy and dying. We no longer use those methods in the military, nor should we rub rocks together and live in caves as clans. Raw stories make us evolve.

The first step in the process to master a six-hour baseline of your life is to learn the three methods of honoring your word and never giving up. The story is merely the context for the visceral learning you must go through yourself. Once mastered, these three methods will transform you. Literally the moment you pass through, you will be different than you are right now.

The entire book is a process. Each step-by-step method is transformative. Each method is simple to engage, yet not easy to overcome. And trust me when I say, "not easy." You have to pass through each by doing it from beginning until complete. You cannot hack the system. You cannot get someone else to do it for you. You can instead just get to it and do it. Simple, but not easy!

Each method in the process has to be completed prior to moving on. Be patient, it will take as long as it takes. If you are willing to engage, anyone can achieve a six-hour baseline. That baseline will put you at a level of performance you cannot yet comprehend. The baseline is nonnegotiable.

The first method has three parts: 21 days of overcoming your excuses, facing your fear, and the 24-hour challenge. Oddly enough, over the past six years of training leaders, athletes, and entrepreneurs, I have witnessed many people attempt the three methods to honor your word and never give up. Few quit in the first seven days. Some completed the three in 30 days. The rest have taken from one month to six months to make it through.

The first method is the simplest and was not intended to be so difficult. However, most people are so ego driven they refuse to kill off their excuse engine. To truly honor your word, you will have to overcome all your reasons and excuses and do what you said you would do. Sadly, we all have excuses that keep us from our own greatness. Honor your word or honor your excuse, the choice is yours! You must see for yourself how you use excuses to get out of doing your life. And, you must honor your word for 21 days straight, without interruption.

My experience in training men and women, SEALS and snipers alike, validates the notion of a 21-day cycle of learning new skills. Twenty-one days of simple activity to carve out a new way of doing anything.

With the acquisition of the most primal skill known to man, honoring your word and never giving up, you must do all 21 days. You must force yourself to do the simple activities to expose your own particular excuses. The real intent of this experience is to expose your excuses and reasons and then, in the face of those believable excuses, do what you promised.

These various excuses are nothing if not believable. There are books written about your excuses to convince you not to do what you said. Often the experience is rather comical watching people deal with excuses. You will find them to be subtle, seductive, and believable. If you let them run your life like they currently do, you are stuffed into a rut. You will find you have constructed a world around you to prove your excuses are more powerful than just saying you are going to do something and executing on that thing.

It takes 21 days to kill off your excuses and reasons and change the environment around you that supports your excuses. Stop excusing yourself from being the person you want to be and just go do what you said you would do. Honoring your word is more effective and much easier as it entails much less drama.

The First 21-Day Evolution

We perform really well when our system is turned on and in motion during the day and is shut down properly every evening. What I didn't realize is that the skill isn't being taught unless you are on a high-performance team or your parents are on point and accountable. In order to show the value of honoring your word and not giving up, I want you to learn the skill of turning on the human system. The method, again, is simple . . . but not easy.

Most of us have a human system that has never intentionally been turned on and, clearly, has never been turned off every day. You, as the driver of this human system, must learn to intentionally turn it on and off every day to succeed.

36

The method will only take 15 minutes in the morning and 15 minutes at night. The first thing you do after waking and the last thing before lying your head down for sleep. Fifteen minutes to turn on and 15 minutes to shut down the human system.

The two-part method is to sequentially turn on the functional parts of the human machine:

Three Simple Things: Spiritual Baseline

1. Morning Action

- Do push-ups, sit-ups, and squats: move every muscle and joint. During week one, do 10 of each; in week two, do 20; and conclude in week three with 30 of each.
- Turn on all five senses: move your eyes through every focal plane; listen for three sounds; smell something pleasant; taste something pleasant; run something with texture, like a hairbrush or a sponge, over your skin.
- Drink eight glasses of water throughout the day.

2. Night Action

- Do the same before bed for 21 days straight.

3. Excuses

- On a notepad, write down the time and every excuse or reason that comes up and makes you want to stop.

It's a simple method I call "the awakening." You will find reasons to excuse yourself very graciously from doing it. You will either come up with a reason in the first week, you will simply forget in the second week, or worse, you will believe your excuses in the third week and quit. You will most likely quit on honoring your word. This first 21-day challenge will show you what is causing you to fail in all areas of your life.

As you prepare yourself for either a 21-day easy learning experience or a six-month tranche of excuses that seduce you into oblivion, the four most noted excuses are as follows. Maybe seeing them written prior to engagement will help.

- This is too painful

- This is stupid

- My spouse/lover/friend doesn't support me

- I forgot

Clearly, pain can be believable. Pain, once used as an excuse, will always stop you.

Saying "this is stupid" has destroyed more endeavors than any excuse known to mankind. What you may not realize is that there is always a point in time when what you are doing is just stupid and makes no sense. You will ask, "Who in their right mind would keep doing this?" or say, "I cannot keep doing this." Overcoming "this is stupid" will be the most important aspect of your life. If you don't overcome this conversation, I can personally promise you one thing: you will stay right where you are in life with the same complaints and reasons and blame everyone but your own choices. "This is stupid" excuses you from change, from taking a step, and from success.

The other seductive excuse to not honor you word is the lack of support from a spouse. Without knowing the outcome of the intimate nature of spousal support, most spouses negatively impact the drive of their loved one. Neither spouse really intends to destroy the other, yet even a sideways look or a scoff of being inconvenienced will derail the one trying to honor their word. Get on board or just tell your spouse openly they don't have your support. I highly recommend being your spouse's cheerleader and always supporting. Unfortunately, the opposite is the reality, due to the fear of being great and a complete lack of understanding what it truly means to be in a relationship. We'll discuss relationship later.

The final of the top four reasons to quit that I have encountered is the most surprising. To make matters worse, it doesn't seem like an excuse. The reality of the excuse "I forgot," is that everyone, everywhere uses it. You will forget to do the simple thing you agreed to do. It doesn't seem to matter how weighty or simple the thing is. We forget to turn off the stove and burn the house down. We forget to fill the tank with gas and run out of gas when least convenient. We forget to say hi and cause unintended ripples in the experience of life for others. In the 21-day challenge, most people forget to do one of the promised things in the last three days. And have to start over. That reality is the life people lead.

The power of the 21-day challenge to honor your word and never give up is that once you stop giving credence to your excuses, once you carve out doing three simple things for 21 days, your life is now moving in the direction you spoke into existence. You are now capable of replicating the experience of doing what you said you would do. Nineteen days is not enough. Twenty days and "I am good" will not be sustainable. Transform your life in twenty-one days. And that is very powerful.

Facing Fear Challenge

The second trial I recommend to honoring your word is to deal openly with fear. Fear is a crippling emotion. Fear is designed to prevent the weak, inexperienced you from engaging the thing that makes you afraid. When fear is present, its effect works 100 percent of the time. Fear stops you.

Ironically, fear can always be overcome by experience and action. But you must act in the face of fear by doing what you are afraid of doing. You must cast off what you think about fear and face it. There is no other way.

Take for instance the most common fears: fear of public speaking, fear of rejection, fear of getting hurt, fear of failure. The fear of public speaking prevents a great many people from succeeding in business. Fear of rejection prevents many of us from asking the question or trying something new. Fear of getting hurt prevents pretty much everyone from venturing off the normal paths we are on in health or in business or in relationships. Fear of failure stops people from even trying something new or hard.

Fear keeps us where we are: doing the same thing over and over and over again.

The method to overcome and openly deal with fear is practical and important to learn. I have taken hundreds of people through this simple lesson in fear and have seen the same result. The result of dealing with fear is action. Through action, all things become available.

I have noticed that once you learn the lesson of dealing with one fear, you can easily apply that same method to dealing with any fear you might have. The most visceral fear to overcome is the fear of falling. I ask you to overcome your fear of heights by rappelling and climbing a 100-foot cliff.

Obviously get a professional climber who is certified to teach and safely take you through the climbing experience. We insist on the safety mechanisms you must have to climb. Still, you must still face your fear and do the climb. Mitigating risk doesn't alleviate fear prior to taking action and doing the thing you are afraid of doing. I can tell you a thousand times how to rappel and climb and even show you, but in that last moment before you actually get to it, you have to overcome your personal fears. You have to hook up and step off. You have to take the action. You have to look down and overcome your fear. You have to climb back up and feel your hands about to slip off. You have to face the possible experience of slipping and falling a short distance and then trying again.

In that moment, or all moments of being gripped by fear but taking action anyway, what happens to fear? Fear disappears once you take action. It literally stops.

What would your life be like if you learned to take action in all the things you are afraid of doing?

24-Hour Challenge

The third iteration, and the most important method of honoring your word and never giving up, is the 24-hour challenge. During the 24-hour challenge, you simply walk at whatever speed you want for 24 hours. The impact is profound. The simple act of just walking for 24 hours forces you to either honor your word and walk or honor every outside circumstance pressuring you and quit. The act of eating and drinking and taking care of yourself and even resting is not easy. You have to feel each step. You have to feel yourself be tired and maybe nauseated. You have to listen to your reasons and excuses and, if you do it in a group, hear other's excuses as well. I call this "the battle against the demons within."

Honoring your word to keep moving will become increasingly difficult because of the lack of experience most of us have in overcoming our internal demons. The rules are simple:

1. Walk for 24 hours.

2. Rest no more than 10 minutes before walking again.

3. Eat and drink as much as you can.

Following these simple rules for 24 hours is a profound experience. I have conducted dozens of 24-hour challenges. Through rain, cold, dry, hot, blisters, and whatever the world throws at us, I show people the method of honoring your word for 24 hours.

Why on earth would I suggest 24 hours? The answer may shock you. Because with freedom and abundance comes decay. The human condition in America, due to abundance, has lost the skill of physical and mental endurance. I am not talking running endurance or high-level athleticism. I am talking the ability to endure the battle within against our excuses for a long time. We, as a nation, have succumbed to excusing ourselves because this inner voice, which we have had no real experience with, now runs the show. It says stop; we stop. It says cheat; we cheat. It suggests fear; we disengage. The internal dialogue, this battle with your demons, has all but vanished in American society. Without this battle being waged and won, we are left with blame, entitlement, and a fragmentation of our souls in the form of sexism and racism and business failure.

In 24 hours, all that ceases. You quiet your storm, you stop blaming, you stop thinking you are due something you didn't work for and, most graciously, you stop seeking differences in others. By actually doing the 24-hour challenge, your ability to see how honoring your word and never giving up causes a shift in you.

Having completed multiple 24-hour challenges with committed clients willing to experience their own self-imposed limits, a few points regarding limitations and foundational principles have emerged. Many of my preconceived notions of what actually stops people from achieving their own goals have been shattered, while some new ideas expose the realities of the human potential to succeed. Each 24-hour challenge pushes my limits and endears me to those willing to press past their own stopping points.

The first attempt went as well as you might expect. I walked it solo. I talked myself out of it when the weather got cold. And I drove home trying to form a story as to why I just couldn't complete it. And trust me, the story was an ingenious fabrication of what happened and didn't happen in order to convince my family it wasn't possible. And my wife, Stacy, after hearing my grand tale said, "So you didn't prepare and take the right clothing and you quit." After a short tantrum on my part, I learned the first two lessons of the 24-hour challenge. These two lessons when translated into everyday life change outcomes immediately.

Lessons one and two are:

We underprepare for a hard life.

We can construct an elaborated story around quitting to convince anyone the thing we tried wasn't possible.

On the second attempt I once again went solo and began the walk with a fever. I was resolute to complete it in spite of the fever. But at the 20-hour mark, I could hardly stand up without falling . . . and I quit once again.

Enter lesson three: *Don't do hard things alone. Isolation destroys humans.*

The third attempt I finally completed. Four of us started it, and at the end I was the only one to walk the last four hours. I certainly didn't want to, because it seemed stupid. I could have quit, because it was painful. I had forgotten to drink enough and was paying the price for the stupidity of that excuse. And my friends who started were really not supportive.

Lesson four crystallized: *The last few steps or last moments of attaining a goal make no sense, are stupid and the mind is thoroughly convinced completing it makes no difference.*

Those four rules have now been etched in stone for me. Such profound lessons are lost in the unconscious grind of everyday life. Learning the lessons strikes the spark lost in life and highlights the value of honoring your word and never giving up. Each 24-hour challenge allows participants the opportunity to learn these lessons. So what will you do?

Will you approach today and tomorrow with a never give up mindset? Will you make a vow to yourself to honor your word?

To honor your word, don't go at it alone. Everyone struggles, whether you're the CEO of a multimillion-dollar company or a father or mother with a new family or a high school student. These leadership principles only work if you don't go it alone.

Don't build a story around failure and sell the copyright to your family. Isolation from others is destructive, and isolation is the enemy of success. As you embark on your journey one step at a time, remember to honor your word to yourself and others. It may not make sense at times, but the hard times never do.

And no matter what you attempt to accomplish, toward the end of it, you will unravel, and even accomplishing it won't make any sense at all.

Simple, but not easy! The three lessons cannot be read and miraculously become a foundation. You cannot learn to honor your word by reading or watching. No matter how long it takes you to complete all three, do it! Without this foundation built on honoring your word and never giving up, all else built on top will crumble.

What would you do if you learned these three lessons?

The Method: The three tests are yours to endure and do. You must pass through all three to construct the foundation needed to build a non-negotiable baseline.

1. *Twenty-one days to carve out something new in life and dig the foundation.*

2. *Face your fear. Do it often in order to pour the foundation.*

3. *Success takes 24 hours of constant movement to set the foundation.*

CHAPTER TWO

Chasing Your Dragons

Simple but Not Easy

*The Process: Finding something big enough
to pursue so that you are consumed by it.*

The most important question of all: What do you want? Are you so committed that you can smell it, taste it, feel it? Have you made it who you are? Successful people leave clues to their success. Your job is to identify the successful people and follow their clues. If you are committed to a goal that is big enough to consume you, you will find a way to do this. Make no mistake—it won't be easy. We all need help. When you begin to learn the processes and methods at the beginning and end of each chapter, your outcomes will shift. I hope that my story of working with an ultrarunning coach provides some clues that you can follow to chase your dragons.

The first month of retirement from the SEAL teams will remain the hardest—emotionally, physically, and spiritually—of my life. We had nothing to hold on to that was familiar. It felt like we, I, didn't matter. As I was informed by other retired SEALs, "The SEAL teams are like a bucket of water. As long as your hand is in the water, you can splash and move the water and effect change, and it feels powerful. As soon as you take your hand out, you can never put it back in to impact any change. If you hold on to the bucket, it will deform your mind and body and make you bitter and resigned."

The whole effort to start over in unfamiliar territory and the ensuing years of relentless effort to raise a family, stay physically fit, build a business of training leaders to thrive in chaos, and remain spiritually available crystalized in my mind to document the entire process so that my family and country could use what I have learned as a map to success. Knowing full well the burden to be authentic to the details would literally expose every weakness and failing I would encounter. In the SEAL teams, everyone, and I really mean *everyone*, fails and breaks down every training cycle and every mission, because in real combat weaknesses exposed become the things you and the team can work through. But they are rarely shared outside the team and never shared with the enemy.

While literally standing on the edge of this cliff of transitioning from being at the "top of my game" to starting completely over with no money and no clear path to support my family, I decided my kids and family deserved to know the truth about warriors coming home to a place unfamiliar and alone. My family deserved my reality, however ugly and brutal war is, hiding reality from your family is really the sin of the fathers.

Through years of living and operating in the SEAL teams, I had learned many valuable skills and processes regarding staying prepared (both mentally and physically) while waiting for the next big thing. The priority of all men is to remain constantly physically available to deal with and endure the unbearable next minute. And, to that end, I began the committed daily ritual of waking up early, preparing my mind and body so that I could endure the challenges to come.

The bitter truth about fitness is that fitness is threefold. Physical fitness is an oxymoron in that physical is only one component; maybe that is why so many people can be sold a trendy program that only deals with one of the three aspects. Physical pursuit, if that is what we should call it, is simple, but not easy: mindset, physical activities, and diet.

One of my most difficult challenges in this process of constantly starting over in life while diligently remaining true to fitness has been keeping it simple and the actions nonnegotiable. Because the truth is that your basic actions literally have to be nonnegotiable and simple to do in the midst of all the chaos and seemingly urgent crises that pop up. I have learned by experience and by observing the downtrodden this simple truth about physical fitness: "Never negotiate with food, the weather, or how you feel. They will always win. Just go do it!"

The simple part of physical and mental fitness is to write down the goal, write down the coaches and team of people who will help, and to write down the exact daily plan. The not easy part is to actually to do the three simple things. I began my retirement from the SEAL teams with this physical plan, and in order to succeed as a father and a husband, I literally wrote it down and shared it with my family. Then I put in on the refrigerator and signed my name to it.

My Baseline

1. I am an ultramarathon runner.

2. My goal is to complete the Pacific Crest Trail 50-miler in May.

3. I need to focus on form and endurance. I need to let go of frustration and disappointment with my pain and back and leg injuries. I need to push my limits once a week. I need to get a mentor.

4. My running partner is Tamara. My lifting partner is Pete. My flexibility partner is Stacy. I will engage my massage therapist, Nikki. I will engage my ultramarathon coach, Serge. I will engage my dietician, Molly.

5. My overall plan is to run 30 miles a week for two weeks, then add 10 miles a week for two weeks. Lift twice a week. Swim once a week. Get one massage a week. Call coach twice a week. My baseline three simple things I must accomplish every day and

pay myself for are run for one hour, stretch for 20 minutes, and drink 10 glasses of water.

6. I am doing this because I said I would do it.

Complexity of Retirement

After the first morning's run when I arrived back at home, Stacy sat there in the kitchen waiting. She always has a way of showing up when needed. "Thom, since I have seen you prepare for SEAL training and combat, I knew I had to be ready for the first morning's letdown," she said as she handed me a cup of coffee. "For some reason that escapes me, you always have a problem in the beginning," she said, laughing again as she turned to sit down and begin the listening to me question myself. "All right, let's hear it."

"The run was normal," I replied after a sip of coffee. "I just took it easy and tried to not get lost."

"Thom, it is raining outside, and you haven't seen rain in four years. Your knees are bleeding and I heard you grunting as you took off your shoes. So cut the deception and tell me what your body feels like and how many times you questioned the choice to get out of the SEAL teams during the two-hour run," she said in a seemingly disgusted tone.

I literally hate that she knows my mind. I hate that she sees my weaknesses and loathe that Stacy won't let me get away with saying all is okay. "My body feels old. I feel old. I fell twice because I wasn't paying attention to the trail. I couldn't even run a 10-minute mile. All I could think about was we don't have any money," I said, looking down knowing that not saying the real truth would just make it worse.

"So?" is all Stacy said. "Either run or make money or make money running. But don't think about money while running. You taught me that. Don't forget everything you have ever learned. You are no longer in the teams because you knew that being promoted to master chief would mean you could no longer carry a gun. Now, you seem like you are making childish decisions. Please, stop the drama, and find an opportunity to carry that gun again." Stacy paused to get another cup of coffee.

"Take a shower. Then how about you and I talk about scheduling the meetings with the five masters you have to have. I will make breakfast and we will sit down and make plans," Stacy ordered. I walked away, not saying anything and tripped going upstairs. "Thank God, Autumn didn't see that," Stacy scoffed as she disappeared back into the kitchen.

Looking back at the initial planning Stacy and I worked through regarding meeting and interviewing one top person in what became the "Five Pyramids of Human Performance," we had no process to follow other than what I had been taught in my years in the SEALs. I only knew simple truths about success and about learning new skills and executing those new skills. Those simple truths took out all the middlemen, eliminated all the good-idea theoreticians, and expelled all the people who hadn't succeeded. The simple truth about successful people is that success leaves clues. And the only way to know success is to follow the clues straight back to the ones who left the trail. Our sole purpose was to find five chronically successful people in each of the Five Pyramids of Human Performance and convince them to show me what they do to succeed.

As we sat at the table in the kitchen in our new house, the silence was overwhelming. We were silent. We were silent for 45 minutes trying to research success and a list of successful people. In the SEAL teams, if tasked to do something better within the framework of being a SEAL, the answers came rather quickly. If I wanted to shoot faster, I could find the really fast shooters, call them up, bring them to training, and have them teach their techniques. Then we would practice the technique for three weeks before we decided if it was good or bad. We would then incorporate all of it, a portion of it, or none of the newly learned skills into our "bag of tricks."

Yet finding a person who mastered wealth was disgustingly difficult. Many men and women had money, yet few during discovery resembled any person or lifestyle I would want to expose my family to, let alone myself. Many men and women had built businesses multiple times but were fat, divorced, or addicted to some drug. Both Stacy and I, after an hour, got up and walked away from the planning party and were saddened to the reality that for the first time in our adult lives neither of us was inspired by top performers. And I was saddened at the prospect that the two first steps in transitioning from the SEAL teams felt so miserable.

While we sat on the couch both angry and laughing at our amateur effort, I recall mentioning, "Stacy, now I know why so many military people fumble or commit suicide when they retire." Stacy grabbed my hand and said something quite remarkable that remains the anchor of our life to this very day, "Thom, no one cares about drama. Bring home meat, or the family will fall apart. Go hunt dragons!"

"Stacy, I don't know many successful businessmen or women who inspire me. I do know several successful athletes, and as we were diving into the discovery, the notion occurred to me that all success in any pyramid leaves clues. I bet all the clues are the same. That is what I am interested in now: finding the clues," I said.

"I am going to spend a week with one of the top 10 ultrarunners and find the clues," I said as I gave her a list of the top 10. The truth I knew about athletes of all sports is that they simply cannot discuss what they know. I would have to go run and spend a majority of the day watching and doing what they do to learn. I dreaded the prospect of trying to convince one of them to allow me their time. But full-on engagement was the only way I knew. Reading and studying from afar just wasn't my way. Going all in, getting 100 percent involved, is the only way. The only issue was "How do I convince them?"

The thoughts of the morning played on my mind as the house began to awaken. Seeing each child come downstairs, groggy and stumbling, and run directly to Stacy and me for a hug then to the couch for what we called the morning nap heightened my sense that all a child needs is two parents and a safe place to grow. All the past stresses of the SEAL teams where each day was a new "sharpening of the knife" day, and where staying on top was critical, sort of bleed away as I realized my new course in life was to protect my kids.

Stacy and I discussed as much in the kitchen as we made bowls of cereal for the kids. "Thom, I think you overdramatize most things! "Our marriage has always been to protect the kids and our family. Isn't that why you went into combat?"

The conversation made sense to Stacy. And on the corner of my thoughts, protection made sense. But I couldn't quite tell Stacy the truth about my going into combat. As I ruminated with the reasons, simply saying to Stacy "I went to combat because I liked it" seemed the wrong thing to say. Wrong in the sense that if I said it that plainly, she would not feel wanted and important. So I kept the thoughts of combat to myself, with no way to share the truth without offending my family.

The following week was filled with the same daily events and same empty thoughts about my value. I have to admit the assessment of my own value was the worst part of retirement. Couple that with the VA losing my retirement pay for the next three months, and triple that with my mentors telling me not to get a job but to spend time and energy discovering my success truths. That triple threat made the first part of leaving the SEAL teams the hardest mental challenge of my life.

"Breaks come to those who hammer" has been my motto since I was 16, and with that mindset my first break came from a runner willing to spend four days with me. I had finally convinced him by offering money. The initial intent was for him to show me all the things he does to be at the top in the ultrarunning community and for me to have permission to take notes. I found it odd he wanted money for some reason yet realize now that many people think time is worth money. I do not think time has a monetary aspect to it; outcome has a price, but not time.

So off I went to California to spend four days with a runner. Stacy and the kids knew I must go, yet the kids didn't understand. They didn't understand why I had to leave since I had been gone for 270 days a year their entire life. They didn't understand it at all. Their emotional response made me question why as well. The long flight didn't make the thought of abandoning the kids for a few days running in the mountains any easier. Yet I had given my word to my mentor and at some point in life, you either honor your word to people or choose to live with that dishonor.

Submit to the Master

My initial thoughts and points I wanted to resolve regarding masters in the five pyramids seemed simple enough to me as I wrote them down during the flight.

1. How much time each day do they spend perfecting their craft?

2. What do they actually do on a daily basis?

3. What is the mindset that makes them unique?

4. Is what they do learnable?

5. Is anything similar across the five masters?

Like most events in my life, what I expected to happen got completely turned upside down rather quickly. The whole experience reminded me of surf passage in the SEAL training, where everything is going well until the huge breaker flips your boat and you are in the water praying for a way out.

Day One

We met for breakfast for the sole purpose of seeing what a top runner eats and maybe what a top runner thinks about before a day of running. For some reason, I expected a strict diet. Some idea inside of me always thinks great people do things differently than the rest. And this morning the first minefield, of my own creation, was assuming there was a diet system or hack top ultrarunners use. I sure wished there had been one, but alas, he ate rather simply. There was no order of non-fat almond milk or goat cheese laced in Himalayan salt and beef.

In response to my question mid meal about what he eats, he simply laughed. "I don't eat sugar because it makes me feel terrible and makes my belly feel bad. I eat real food as much as possible. I like to eat and learned long ago that to run long distance and enjoy the process, food had better be fun to eat and make you feel better. All that processed, packaged stuff doesn't really work. It makes people feel important but doesn't make me personally run faster or longer," he said. "Thom, just eat real food and drink a lot of water." Point in fact, we had two eggs over medium, bacon, coffee, orange juice, and toast.

"I expected something different for breakfast from a top ultrarunner," I said once we got into the vehicle to head up to the mountain toward the trail and first run.

"Thom, food is the simple part of the running equation. Let me explain! Fat is good for you as a runner because it satiates your cravings and lasts a long time. Carbs, real food carbs, give you quicker energy. Protein, real protein, repairs all the damage we are about to do to our organs and muscles and seems to give you sustainable energy. Hydration, as in water, is the real key to endurance running for about a thousand reasons that are going to become very clear over the next four days. There are three basic types of salts, and each noticeably impacts different parts to the body. Table salt retains fluid in your body. Potassium salt helps your muscles relax or recover after contraction. Calcium salts help the muscles contract. The key is to keep them in balance, because we are clearly going to make everything go out of whack, and if we don't eat and drink correctly, you will be lying on the side of the trail," he said, laughing. "I have lain on the side of the trail many times because I didn't pay attention to simple basic rules of nutrition and hydration.

"Simple rules are hard to follow," he continued as we arrived at the trail parking lot. "Follow these simple rules today for the next five hours of running. Drink every 15 minutes five swallows of water. Eat

200 calories every 30 minutes. Don't let your heart rate get above 160 while running. Yes, walking is what we do a lot in ultrarunning," he said so calmly I thought he was making an off-the-cuff joke. "Are you going to write those rules down?" he asked me.

"I would, but you lost me at five hours of running," I said, laughing. "How are we going to run five hours is my sticking point."

"You came to run, so let's get to it," he said with a chuckle.

Yet I could tell he seemed to wonder why I had come. "Never ask how to do something this hard," he said. "Just ask what we are going to do and where we are going to go and the duration. If you are committed, you will find a way how to do this. If you are not committed, you will keep asking how we are going to do it," he said matter-of-factly, like it was known that amateurs ask how to do things.

So I wrote down the rules in my notebook, documenting we were going to run/walk up Grey's and Torey's Peaks in five hours. I put on my shoes and grabbed my pack and food and water. I began to realize I was over my head in more ways than I could comprehend. So many things seemed to be missing, such as warm up and stretching, and a safety plan of any kind.

The weather was 50 degrees, and the top of the mountain still had snow. He wore shorts and a loose long-sleeve shirt and a short sleeve underneath. And he stuffed a warmer jacket in his small pack with his food and water. I, however, wore winter hiking clothes and was packed heavy with food and water. I packed like a Navy SEAL.

"Hey, check my pack. Make sure I have the right stuff in there," I said, more concerned than wanting guidance. "And what if we get rained or snowed on? Are we taking enough clothes?"

"I gave you guidance already," he said, looking at my gear and laughing. "Do you always overcomplicate things?" We both laughed. "Take what you think you need. You will learn only by doing. And don't get injured and, listen closely, run faster if you are cold. Deal with problems early and often, or they will get worse."

I always laugh at what "masters" say, keep it simple, deal with things as they arise, and move faster. The saying in the SEALs is KISS, Keep It Simple Stupid. I am very sure it was simple in his mind with all of those experiences, yet running for five hours for the joy of it didn't register with me. Admittedly, I spend 23 years doing something that was fun and joyous for me in the SEALs, but my brain was having issues with running in the cold for pleasure.

Relief came when my new running coach said, "Here is what I am going to do today during training. The first hour is practicing eating and drinking and running only the flat sections. The next three hours I am planning on running for 15 minutes and walking for two minutes. Then, in the final hour, we should cool down and jog easily downhill." With that, he turned and began to walk up the trail.

Lessons One: Run Your Own Race

If you have ever hiked or ran through the Sierras in California, then you know the drill. The trailhead parking lot is always well-kept. Probably because no one drives two hours into the backcountry to hike for five hours. The air that morning was dry, yet cold enough to see your breath. We parked at 5,000 feet of altitude. I could feel the difference in my breathing almost immediately.

The trails in the Sierra, I have to admit, are well-kept. The decomposed granite is coarse to walk on, and the sound of your shoes crunching on the trail somehow just makes sense. The whole of the environment feels like you *should* be on the trail. Each turn in the trail is visually stunning, and in the distance you can see over the mountains. To the west was the ocean and to the east was some other mountain. I felt good and thought the day would be great.

All this wonderment stopped as my new running coach started to jog. The trail didn't seem flat to me. I picked up the pace. I looked at my Garmin watch and it read a 15-minute mile. Then I looked up and my newfound friend was gone. I wasn't sure how it was possible for him to be gone, like completely gone, so quickly, yet he had disappeared up the trail. Like any good frogman, I picked up my pace for the simple reason that I felt competitive. I ran faster and faster, hoping to catch him. After 30 minutes of running at a 9-minute mile pace, I slowed, to wonder if I had missed a turn. I began to wonder if he had just taken off and ditched me and taken the money.

Oh, the thoughts of "what am I doing here" and "did I really just get taken" weren't the only things I was dealing with. I wasn't thinking about running, that was clear. With my temper rising, I turned the corner and could see the trail curved down and to the right. And much to my surprise, there he was, sitting on a tree stump, drinking water.

The 100 yards of walking up to him with all that "what the heck" about to burst out must have been palpable. He stood and shook my hand. "Thom, the first lesson of ultrarunning is run your own race. And keep eating and drinking no matter what happens," he said with a calm matter-of-fact expression. "Did you drink and eat?"

I looked at him for a moment as I realized he was teaching me something not just out for a day of running. "Nope, I was trying to keep up with you and forgot."

"Sit down and eat and drink now, and rest until your heart rate comes down to 120 beats per minute," he said with no apparent disgust.

On the one hand, I always love to be in the mountains doing hard things and enjoying the movement. And, on the other hand, I was worried about wasting my money and realized I wasn't the athlete he was. The weighing of enjoyment and not fitting in must have caught his attention.

"Thom, if I may take the liberty to coach you for a minute. I am only here coaching you because you were a SEAL and you are trying to figure out what is next for you. I am not here at this point to teach you about ultrarunning because you haven't made the important decision to actually be an ultrarunner," he said frankly.

"Being unsure of who you are and what you want to do next is a dangerous place, not only as an ultrarunner but as a human being."

He paused to see how I was taking on the coaching. Needless to say, I was listening.

"I am an ultrarunner. Period! I run because it is who I am. I sometimes run fast, sometimes slow, often times longer than I intended, but I run," he said, smiling.

"What I don't do is compare myself to other runners or bring my uncommitted mind on a run." He leaned forward and poked me in the shoulder. "Make the choice of who you are before you try something this hard. Ultrarunning can kill the uncommitted."

I sat there on the stump, dumbfounded. Maybe my initial analysis of anyone outside the SEAL community being on point and professional was completely wrong. Moreover, I was more befuddled by the fact that he knew what I was going through, which had nothing to do with running.

"Well," I began, "here is my truth: I don't want to be obsolete. I don't want to feel like all my life's work in the SEAL teams was for nothing." I really wanted him to understand where I was coming from and was dealing with. "And I hate doctors telling me I will never run again because my bulging disks are too risky to run on."

I felt like a stupid, young, complaining child the moment I said it. I felt like I had puked all over a new pair of expensive leather shoes and the owner of the shoes was going to go nuts.

He laughed. "Dude, run or don't run. No one cares but you. And that is the truth of it. All that mental trash is exhausting. Pain is for sure in ultrarunning, whether you are injured before a run or get injured during a run. No one cares. All I have to say is runners run," he said, still laughing.

He was right. My experience, all that I had learned in the SEAL teams, at this moment was completely thrown aside as mental trash. I chuckled with him. "That, I can do," I said as I continued to laugh. "Pain I am comfortable with, yet I somehow forgot that simple truth."

"All right, let's reset and first apply the first skill of ultrarunning. Over the next hour, I ask you to eat and drink as we discussed and keep your heart rate below 160. I will stay with you, and you watch what I do," he said as we began to move again.

The next hour was rather uneventful. We moved up the trail and simply applied the basics he had mentioned. It was that simple.

We stopped to sit and rest near a small stream crossing, which led to what appeared to be an uphill climb into a bowl near the peak. We discussed the basics of the past hour and how the basics are not negotiable in training. The added bonus of having an accomplished master in his craft is how simple his mind makes everything.

The next two hours was to keep the basics in play and add what he called "single point of focus." The explanation was brilliant. "Uphill running and downhill running are harder than running the flats. On the flats your thoughts can be random, but on the hills a scattered mind will get you injured. I have learned over the past 10 years of running that the most important thing to think about is posture or form running. Make sure your mind keeps thinking and forcing your whole body back into good form. Add focus thoughts and actually good form running to the basics on the uphill and downhill. I am going to do this next section at my pace. You do it at your pace and we will meet at the top," he coached, and I listened. With that, he was off.

The feeling of elation when reaching the top of a mountain is always perfect. No matter how rough the climb, a small period of "Hey, this is cool" always arrives. Even in combat, once a big firefight is over, the same period of "Hey, this is cool" comes. As we sat there, he completely dry and rested and me soaked and still out of breath, we talked about focus and if I had kept up with my eating and drinking and heart rate.

"Well," I said, "I did keep up with the intake, but five minutes into the climb my heart rate spiked above 160. Unless I wanted to completely stop, even walking pushed the heart rate. So I just walked and stopped and walked and stopped."

"The form focus I have to figure out." I paused wanting his coaching but didn't get it immediately. "Focusing on body form only lasted about five steps. Then I would worry about heart rate or how far I had to go. But for five seconds it was easier."

"Good," he merely said. "Focus is always short lived. Just keep coming back to it even though it doesn't last long."

While I caught my breath and let my muscles catch up with all the energy lost going uphill, he observed, "Okay, downhill running is a nimble foot and strength problem. Add to your mental thoughts quick feet or nimble feet and I will meet you at the stream again." Off he went.

Up until that point in my life, I thought downhill was easier. Maybe it was easier in my mind, thinking at least I don't have to hike up. Maybe it was easier because heart rate always comes down during the downhill trek. Yet I quickly realized downhill running requires more muscle strength than uphill. My legs burned much worse than on the uphill. My toes were jammed into the front of my shoes and hurt for the entire hour. When I turned the corner and saw him sitting alongside the stream with his feet in the water, I at least knew it was a universal issue. "Downhill running hurts," he said.

As I flopped down next to him, he merely asked, "Did you eat and drink?" I replied yes. "What is your heart rate now?" I looked and replied, "120." "Did you focus on form?" I said, "Not as much because I was focused on thigh pain and toe pain."

We sat silently for a time and let the cool stream water take the edge off the foot pain. I looked at his feet and had to admit his toes looked horrid. He had no toenails.

I pointed to his feet and said, "You aren't making a living as a foot model, are you?"

He said, "Nope, and I don't really care to. It is the price of not focusing on nimble footfalls on the downhill and not dealing with pain as soon as I feel it. They are always a reminder to pay attention to simple things and not have pride.

"Now I want you to apply everything we have discussed today over the next 90 minutes it will take to get back to the parking lot. Just focus on form and nimble feet when needed and eat and drink and don't let heart rate get above 160. See you at the parking lot," he said.

The rest of day one was enjoyable except for the pain. Seeing the parking lot as I rounded the last bend reminded me of seeing the helicopter arrive to extract us out of some godforsaken combat engagement. Similar to the fact that no matter how bad that last bit had been, all the pain goes away in the end.

Oddly enough, during the ride down the mountain, I expected a deep didactic review of what he had discussed on the trail. He simply ate some extra food and drank the rest of the water he had. When he was done, he suggested I do the same. We talked about stretching after dinner and he advised me not to eat dessert that night.

Second Lesson: Master the Basics

We had a later start on day two. He had an obligation in the morning, and we drove up separately. I arrived 30 minutes early in order to stretch and prepare for what I anticipated to be a harder day. My feet were rather stiff, and so were my knees and lower back. My lower back always is stiff due to all the hard landings from jumping out of airplanes and all the helicopter hard landings in Afghanistan years before. As I stretched, the thoughts of "what am I doing here" bloomed as they always tend to do when I am alone. Isolation is not a friendly experience.

He pulled in on time and, as a matter of routine, got his running items in order and warmed up without talking. My impression of masters is they don't talk about random things very much. I know when I was on the top of my game in the SEALs, conversation of any kind was a distraction. Instead of talking, I watched and shadowed what he was doing simply to gain experience and get a return on my investment.

The weather was simply gorgeous. No clouds! Seventy degrees. Some families were setting out on the trail before us, and more were arriving. I always find the experience of watching families enjoy the freedoms I helped provide to be rather rewarding. This morning was one of those times.

"Okay, Thom," he said as we walked over with his running pack and water bottles. "Nothing new today. I want to remind you to eat every 30 minutes and drink every 15 minutes. I want you to focus on form and focus on nimble foot placement. That is really all running is. I want you to understand these basic aspects because until you fully ingrain the basics, nothing else I can tell you will have any effect on your running."

"Can you run slower for the first hour and demonstrate the basics to me? I want to watch you do what seems easy to talk about, but I am finding these things you are asking to be not so easy to do on the trail," I asked as a matter of principle.

"Perfect," he said. "Follow me and do what I do when I do it until we get to the stream crossing. I am going to stop every time I drink and eat, and I'll also stop every time I drift off from focusing on form running."

Running with a really, I mean *really* good runner is an education in and of itself. I had had similar experiences in the SEALs with master shooters and master tacticians. Oftentimes, watching and letting the masters show you how they do it produced better results than talking about it. And I knew a truth that most masters cannot talk about what they do as well as they can just do it. Running and watching and seeing if I could do exactly what he was doing and when he was doing it was the goal in my mind.

The first hour up to the stream crossing before the hard uphill turned out to have many more stops on the trail than I had expected. We stopped rather often because he wanted to make the point that even he couldn't retain perfect running form or mental-form focus for very long. I found it both distracting and interesting. Distracting because I could never settle into a running cadence because we stopped every 90 seconds for about 2 seconds. Interesting because I didn't realize he got distracted so quickly.

As we pulled up to the stream crossing and sat and rested before the huge uphill, he smiled and said, "Form is fleeting isn't it? But if you don't practice stopping when you lose form, you will actually spend a lot of time running out of form and out of focus. The practice of focus at this stage and for the rest of the run up the hill is to notice and stop when form falls apart," he said very calmly. "If all I show you is that point, and you work on the mental and physical aspect of getting form back into focus, you will be a really good runner and enjoy the runs and not get injured. Most people spend hours running not focused on anything.

"I had intended to leave you here, but I like what you are doing and that you pay attention." He stood up and offered a new plan. "On the uphill running section ahead, I want you to run in front of me and I am going to keep reminding you how to keep form and remind you to stop if the form is off."

"Good," I said. "Uphill is a struggle because I am out of shape. Any help would be great."

"Wait," he said. "Thinking you are in shape or out of shape is really stupid. Just look at running as how much technique you have and how much energy you have in the tank. In ultrarunning, it doesn't matter if you are in good shape or bad, at some point in the run you will be in what we call the 'pain cave.' There have been times when I could hardly walk. And there have been times when I can run an eight-minute mile up this exact hill. My point is, maintain the basics as a framework to approach every mile and every step. The basics are to eat, drink, and focus on form and nimble feet."

The next two hours flew by. Every time I broke form, he told me to stop and walk for 20 seconds. Every time I stopped to walk, I began to realize that the walking made it easier to get my mind and body to focus again. I also realized my heart rate rarely got above 160 beats per minute. I felt like I walked more than I should have, yet I felt fresher mentally and my legs were not totally "smoked" at the top. I mentioned my desire to run faster and not stop as much.

"Thom, who told you speed is so important?" He looked at me as if I had spoken in a foreign language.

"Well, isn't speed the goal of running?" I asked.

"No, speed is a trap," he said, laughing. "The goal of running ultras is to eat and drink and keep focusing on form and nimble feet as long as you can in any condition that comes up on the trail. Chasing speed will always cause you to make a bad choice."

Stretching and drinking and eating seemed to be the only things I saw him do; they seemed to be all that he did and was concerned with. For the few minutes we lingered at the top of the mountain, the impression I got of him was he was always on point with making sure his body and thoughts were centered around ensuring he could run well.

"You seem to always be taking care of yourself even here at the top," I said. "You don't seem to be concerned with the scenery and other issues."

He laughed as if I had asked a childish question. "When you were in combat, did you look at the opium flowers and think how pretty they were? Did you want to just shake hands with the farmer?" he asked.

"On the way down, I want you to practice what we did on the way up," he said, moving on from the earlier question. "Keep your feet nimble, keep eating and drinking and heart rate low. Make sure you are either focused on form or you stop so that you can focus. I really know that this basic skill is everything."

As he gave me his hand and helped me up to my feet, he said, "This time down, don't stop at the stream, instead go all the way down to the parking lot. I will meet you there. When you get there, I will have questions for you, and I ask you to have questions for me."

And off he ran. This guy loved to run! I have to admit it was fun to watch him run fast on trails that are not known for easy running.

The method of staying on point with drinking five swallows of water every 15 minutes and eating 180 calories every 30 minutes really gases the running engine. I could feel the difference it made on my energy and my ability to think normally. Keeping my heart rate low was the biggest challenge. I had initially blamed it on being overweight and out of shape, yet as I toyed with speed and effort and ensured fuel was going in, the heart rate seemed controllable.

The process of focusing on form did ensure shoulders were loose and knees and ankles and hips were working together. The previous injury in my lower back from a helicopter crash, however, hurt at a level 6 on a 10 scale of pain. The hardest point and the point of losing focus was when pain was more than form. I stopped often because my thoughts would center on back pain and not form.

The entire routine of pain making me stop and walk became the game I was playing: How long could I focus on form before pain overwhelmed me? The routine seemed like a lost cause. Everything revolved around tranches of form/eat/drink/nimble feet, then it all broke down into pain tolerance. Then it simply became a matter of walking until the pain wasn't the only thing in my mind.

All the sights and sounds around me were tertiary to balancing pain and focus. I have to admit I had lost track of time and even where I was on the trail when all of a sudden, I rounded a corner and there he sat in the parking lot on a bench. He rose as I approached.

"Well that was different, it seems," he said. "You are here 45 minutes earlier than I suspected."

During the long run down the mountain, my intent was to reflect on what I learned and make some sort of sense of it. Like most desires in life where you wish for one particular thing, another unexpected thing dominates the time instead. After getting off the back roads that led to the trailhead, the highway was bumper to bumper. The normal 60 minutes to get to my hotel now extended to three hours.

Reflection turned into frustration with idiot drivers, which turned into realizing I had not eaten or consumed any water for three hours. When I finally opened my door to stand up, my muscles and joints clearly had made the choice to reject my offer to move. My feet felt like big fat sponges with needles sticking into my soles; my lower back truly wanted to stay in the sitting position. The price of getting old is paid with buckets of pain and stiffness.

The walk to my room immediately reminded me of what I felt like after Hell Week during SEAL training. Everything hurt, everything felt swollen, and any "willpower" was completely shattered. That second night, the notion of running again in the morning was completely dominated by trying to get my body to recover and forcing my thoughts to stop looking for every excuse to not show up in the morning.

My thoughts were so negative I decided to write them down, and in the morning show them to my coach:

—My feet are too swollen to run safely.

—My lower back is really injured, maybe I should go to the doctor.

—My eyes and lips are swollen—maybe I have a liver or heart condition.

—I am too old for this.

—I am not really built for long distance.

—This is a waste of my time.

When I turned off my alarm in the morning to get up, everything seemed worse. And, on top of all the discomfort, my thoughts were already checked out. For 10 minutes I had completely convinced myself to simply not show up. "I don't owe him anything. He doesn't really care anyway, he got his money. My kids and wife need me home. This is really selfish of me to take four days away from family and just run." I spent 10 disgustingly long, believable minutes talking myself out of running.

I sat there in the darkness of the hotel room and didn't like the person I was becoming in retirement. I didn't like the counterproductive thoughts. I didn't want the rest of my days to be spent avoiding running or even hiking because of the pain. I didn't want all the years of being tough to slide away in the one second it takes to "be" a quitter. I really felt disgusted with who I was devolving into being.

So I stood up and simply said, "For God's sake, just get ready and at least go to breakfast." Sitting there in the hell of my own weak mindset of pain and quitting wasn't me. This weakness wasn't me.

The breakfast didn't make a difference regarding pain and the swelling in my legs. The drive up the mountain was a blur. When I arrived at the trailhead, my coach was there, apparently unaffected by yesterday and how I looked and walked. He merely watched me, waiting for me to speak.

"I feel like death," I stated. "Yet I am here."

"Good" is all he said.

"I want to share my thoughts I wrote down last night as I was looking for ways to excuse myself from running today," I said. As I handed him my notes, I realized that's what he was waiting for.

He took the notes and read them aloud without laughing or looking up at me. For several minutes he reread them and flipped the paper over several times. "Is that all?" he asked.

"My body is not ready for this today, and everything hurts and is swollen," I retorted. "Last night sucked because of it."

He sat and looked at me and smiled. He didn't say anything for a long time. For a moment I actually thought he was going to let me off the hook and suggest it was safest not to run because it would do damage to my old body. Maybe I was still wishing for an exit excuse?

"Runners run. Pain is inevitable. Suffering is for fools. You don't strike me as a fool. Why do you suffer so much?" he asked, actually seeming to want to know that answer.

I had not thought of dealing with pain as a point of suffering. Trying to find an answer and not sound like a fool was actually hard. "Well, I am out of shape and I don't want to do damage," I said. As I spoke I felt like I was throwing a ball knowing it was going to rebound and hit me in the face, but I couldn't stop throwing it.

"This experience of ultrarunning is what separates us from marathon runners. The feeling of being completely broken either in a race or in training is part of it. Battling the broken mind and body by just getting on the trail to make it through the next mile. Just running is really boring. But this battle you are now going through is worth the money, don't you think? Let's battle this together today," he said, standing up and extending his hand to help me up. "Now you know why ultrarunners have a pacer in the latter part of races."

"Okay, this is going to hurt," I said.

"Experience tells me something different. Experience tells me it will hurt more if you don't win this battle. And you will be surprised when, maybe an hour from now, the pain will subside and so will the swelling," he said.

"Thom, as a reminder, ultrarunning today is no different than yesterday. Eat and drink on point like we discussed. Run or walk, making sure your heart rate is less than 160 beats per minute. And focus on form and nimble feet. All this mental suffering and pain is a mere distraction," he said.

The first hour looked like walking. Yet I kept to the basics with his help. The battle was real. The idea that getting to the next bend in the trail or next tree or next rock began to be my focus. Form as a point of reference became secondary in my own head.

Throughout the rest of the day, my simple point of focus was to get to the next tree. Then get to the next and the next. My coach constantly interrupted my own thoughts, telling me to drink and eat or keep my form up or think about nimble feet. Each of his suggestions were met with an apology and a chuckle when I tried to make my feet be nimble. Pain came with every footfall.

I don't recall the top of the mountain nor the two stream crossings from the previous days. I didn't really care where I was or what the weather was doing. Finally, we were at my rental car. I recall being a bit put off that the car was there. I was upset.

"Thom, now I want you to use my stretching pad and lie there with your feet up for 20 minutes," he said, retrieving the ground pad, stretching out, helping me down. And for 20 minutes we stretched. I had realized I had forgotten to do that yesterday. I had completely forgotten to take care of mind and body by stretching and letting the toxins get filtered through my system before sitting in a car. Such a simple basic point of practice, and it completely upended me. After the rest and stretch, we talked about the day of running and learning about ultras.

"Thom, today was real ultratraining. I want to tell you what to take away and what to leave behind. Ultrarunners need help. That is why pacers are allowed. All the pacer does is keep the runner doing the simple basic things and help him from feeling isolated and alone. Takeaway number one," he said.

"Yeah, I can see that because I wouldn't have gone had you not been here," I said, laughing.

"Being in shape and losing weight and working out is helpful to push off what you just went through. But the pain cave or tunnel of despair will come in 99 percent of the races you will do. Expect it and train for it," he added. "That's takeaway number two.

"What I ask you to leave behind is that you are broken and not enough," he said. "Leave the mental weakness on the trail. Takeaway number three. Tomorrow we will do five different workouts. Each you can use to gain the advantage of the specific workout."

That night I ate well and was still in pain and stiff, yet I didn't care. I ran and walked for five hours even though it seemed stupid and impossible. Some of the stuff I had learned in the SEAL teams was still applicable in the world of retirement. For some strange reason I was encouraged that I could use several aspects of being a SEAL in retirement.

The next day we met at a track. The first hour-long track workout was to improve form by going fast. I like to run fast and also knew speed burns calories rather quickly, so I was interested in what he may know about conserving energy while moving fast. The workout was simple: One hour of 200-meter sprints followed by 200-meter walks. Oddly enough, the sprints felt more comfortable than walking. He and I ran side by side the entire time. I always enjoy watching a really good runner run. Even as a SEAL I would go to college track meets just to watch great runners.

"What is the advantage of sprints to endurance running?" I asked.

"Form is the advantage. The body runs with better form when it runs faster. The other advantage is training your mind and body to recover after a hard sprint. And the only way to train your muscles and organs is to do the sprint/walk workout," he said.

The second hour-long workout was stadium running. Sprint up and walk down for an hour. These were the types of workouts we always did in the SEAL teams, so I was familiar with it. Up and down, up and down. I have to admit the delays at the bottom were longer and longer, yet he didn't push to do more.

"This is uphill running, which is all butt muscle and thigh and all heart. The downhill is more important. The muscles need to get used to running downhill. Downhill running training, I think, is what makes your race go well if you are used to it, or it can make you suffer if you neglected to train," he said.

The next hour of ultrarunning workout was again simple. We were to run for 10 minutes and lunge for 10 minutes. He explained that the best training he could offer regarding preparing the legs for the hammer session that ultraracing is, the lunge-jog routine. Very simple, very easy to explain, but very hard to do because my mind could not quite overcome my thigh pain. My thighs felt like they were on fire. When I ran, they felt like wet spaghetti noodles.

The fourth hour felt more like SEAL training. Twenty jumping-jacks, 20 sit-ups, 20 push-ups. The pace was slow. He simply said, "Form is the only thing that matters here." I ached a weird ache, the kind that really is trying to tell you to hide and find a way around doing the training. When the final day ended, we sat together silently.

After a bit of stretching he offered the last bit of coaching: "Run be-cause you want to. Keep running simple. And get help. I look forward to running in a race with you soon." And with that, we shook hands, and he drove away.

Once back at home, once back with family, Stacy and I sat down to discuss the next steps in retirement. The entire notion of retirement turned me off completely. I did not want to *be* retired. Stacy knew not only my health would suffer, but we as a family would suffer, and the kids would not thrive. We discussed as much as she said, "Thom, now you know why I want you to hunt dragons until you cannot any lon-ger. You are intolerable, and I don't find the state of mind you were in very attractive. In fact, it turns me off.

"You will not like my suggestion. I ask your next dragon to be to train other leaders in business how to take ownership of the five areas of life you have centered your life and success on since I have known you," she said, placing the gauntlet on the table.

"I don't even know where to begin. We need money now, not a new business," I said, feebly pushing back.

"No, you need a dragon or a war. Since you can no longer go to war, then trust me, you need an impossible dragon to fight," she said, laughing.

The Method: Commit before you have a solution, then do whatever is required to succeed.

CHAPTER THREE

The Formula

The Process: Establish the link between words and actions.

Is what you say true for you? True to the degree in which what you do is defined by what you say you will do? If you're like most people, you probably think it is. My experience has shown me that what we say, both out loud and in our minds, impacts our outcomes. Sounds simple enough, but it's not always easy to put into practice. We often let our environments or other people dictate our words and actions and thus our outcomes. It's time to kill your excuses and get real about your language. There are formulas for choosing language that impacts success. These formulas are the same for all.

All men and women are fundamentally designed the same way. We all, however, manifest our thoughts and filter our goals through the same preexisting life formula in very different and unique ways. The whole design of human beings is flawless and stunning when you actually uncover the formula in which we all organize our lives. I have yet to encounter even one person not using or being used by this formula in all of the five pyramids of human performance.

After six months of interviews, of actual work, and of combining my experiences with those of others, a pattern began to take shape. Maybe my background of hunting, possibly my times in combat, and actually my desire to always have a "takeaway point for action from everything I do" led me to take the pattern I had witnessed and make a formula.

Patterns that constantly repeat themselves, such as the sun rising or the seasons changing or wake and sleep cycles or breathing or even stock market bull and bear cycles are the fundamental observations to determine. Often, patterns are difficult to unravel and sometimes do not exist at all. Essentially, when patterns are discovered, then an underlying process or formula is always driving them. And that, my friends, is where I found myself: Looking at a formula that drives the pattern of success and of failure.

The pattern exposed a formula, or a way of human engagement, that seemed to be used by the winners, the middle group, and the ones on the bottom. The ones at the top profoundly used every element of the formula, every day, no matter what. The middle ground used most of the formula and often didn't engage at all on certain days. The ones at the bottom seemed to be used by the formula every day, yet the environment around them wrote the formula for them. Nevertheless, the formula actually seemed to run 24 hours a day, whether people knew it or not. I was shocked, period!

The goal in all my activities after leaving the teams was to find something that affected everyone, no matter if they were down and out or up and running. I had to keep asking myself if there was an underlying cause as to what made people win and lose. As the formula emerged the next challenge was to have it validated or totally blown up by professionals. I had learned in the teams to test ideas by seeing if other people had already learned a similar skill or to use the idea in the practical world and have reality destroy it. Many ideas die once they get exposed to the light of reality. But a few work really well. The formula worked really well once exposed to the light of reality. It even survived lawyers and teachers and philosophers.

I was asked to share my experience at a psychology conference in California. I thought it quite humorous to be a man of war and a conservative to fly to California and present an idea in psychology to academia. As my wife and friends would always say, "What is a knuckle-dragging warrior doing in a cerebral conversation about human performance?" The idea was to have them destroy my formula, completely. I literally wanted them to say "Yes we know that already" or "Next, move along."

The audience was 52 psychologists and psychiatrists. The venue was an auditorium with me and the chairperson on stage sitting there using a question-and-answer-based presentation. The topic was "the formula for human performance." In my mind the whole thing wouldn't last longer than 10 minutes, once I cursed or I couldn't answer the first question with high English. I began simply with "My experience with this event we call human life is that we humans are all capable of extraordinary accomplishments, and we all have the capacity in one minute to destroy everything we have ever accomplished."

I paused for an effect that didn't come. No one seemed to know I was there at all and only a few eyes were even looking at me.

"No matter the status of success or the condition of scarcity, I notice an underlying mechanism working extremely well. A preexisting formula that runs everything we do. The formula is driven by internal dialogue or, rather, language itself drives the outcomes."

Second pause for effect. Nothing!

"There are five areas, I call them pyramids of performance, of growth, where the same formula is running and predictably achieving outcomes dependent on the language being used to fill in each line item. More importantly, the formula and process and method to fill it in properly can be learned, with outcomes shifted very quickly."

I didn't need to pause. I was interrupted.

"I am a professor of ontology; would you show us the formula?" a gentleman asked from the top row.

"The formula is predicated on two foundational underpinnings. Meaning to master or get access to shaping the formula, one has to learn these two points first. They are 'honor your word' and 'never give up on honoring your word.' The process takes 21 days to weed out and show how internal dialogue or words dramatically impact performance. I call this process 'killing your excuses.'

"The formula has six parts to it. It is a linear progression formula, meaning you literally have to fill in the blanks from left to right. Let me show you." With that, I proceeded to write out the formula on the white board.

1. Declaration State of Who You Are (must use correct wording)
    a. I AM: Unbreakable, Infinite, Abundant, One, and Connected to All Things

2. Mission Statement or goal statement (must always detail what, where, and, when)
    a. What you are going to accomplish
    b. When you are going to accomplish it
    c. Where it is going to be accomplished

3. Need Statements (tools of performance)
    a. Focus—I need to be on 100 percent or I need to be off
    b. Problem-solving—I need to let go of every emotional attachment
    c. Breakthrough—I need to embrace failure to learn
    d. Mentor—I need to mentor others

4. Accountability Partners Statement (the team you form around you)
    a. Three partners who teach you a new skill and hold you accountable to your actions
    b. Three partners who do actions that are required, and you hold them accountable

5. Detailed Plan of Execution Statement
    a. Must backward plan from two weeks post success back to the day you will start
    b. Must assign a team member to a part of the plan
    c. Must detail time, actions, and resources needed

> d. Must achieve the baseline of three simple things per pyramid that you will do every single day

6. Why Statement

> a. The only answer of any merit or sustainable value is "because I said so."

My friend, the doctor of ontology, calmly said, "Give me an example."

I had anticipated examples. Examples are third party, uncommitted, out-of-context useless tools to discuss topics that no one is committed to resolving. The only way around an example is to deal immediately with the person requesting the example. "No," I said. I stopped and looked at him. "An example will not work for you. Instead, if you are willing, I have a question for you directly."

"Sure, I would be somewhat excited if a Navy SEAL could show me something about human development that I don't already know."

"I can show you *nothing* you don't already know. That was my point up front. Everyone, everywhere already knows the formula and uses it in portions or in totality or is being used by it. I simply have a question that the answer will unfold the formula rather quickly," I said, pausing for effect. I sized him up quickly, because if I stumbled here, I was done. He was mid fifties. He was not athletic, because he was rather heavy for his height, and my years of coaching athletes and sizing up the enemy always comes in handy.

"My question is this: In the pyramid of health, can you run 100 miles?" I asked in a rather straightforward manner.

He actually didn't answer quickly. "My initial response was hell no," he said. "Yet I suspected you anticipated that."

I interrupted, "Can you run 100 miles or not?" I hoped to make him react, like most people do, because reaction always exposes weakness.

"No, I cannot run 100 miles," he said with certainty.

"Good," I said. "That is true for you. So why can you not run 100 miles?" I said as I walked up the aisle to face him.

"Because I am not a runner. And, even if I were, 100 miles is stupid and could cause damage." He clearly knew he wasn't a runner.

I walked up to him and shook his hand, "Thank you for your graciousness. I don't mean to cause disruption. I just find it amazing how quickly you filled in every line item of the formula without even knowing you did."

I remained in front of him and continued. "Like most of us, we fill in the formula out of sequence and out of the false notion that the past or nature informs us of what is possible. Nature is stupid, by the way. Nature just reports or reflects. You immediately jumped to line item six. You answered 'the why' with a weak excuse. Had you answered why with 'because I said so,' I would have been very impressed. Then you filled in the blank of who you are with who you are not. The other line items get filled in with zero, by active omission." I smiled and turned and walked back down the aisle.

"Yet, you think that is true. You actually think you cannot run 100 miles. However, it is not true that you cannot do it. Obviously, people do it. Not so obvious, I bet, that people just like you do it. And I bet most of you are oblivious to the fact that blind people, people with no arm or no leg, do it. I can tell you they start with declaring themselves a runner well before they know how they will accomplish it.

"Then, runners actually have to sign up and pay for the goal," I said, taking a deep, audible breath.

"I do apologize. That question is a setup, most of the time." I turned and looked at him again. "Same question asked differently, what are you great at doing?"

"I love being a professor. My students do really well in my classes, and they learn something valuable in their lives," he said plainly.

I smiled. "How many students do you have?"

"We teach 212 students a year," he replied.

"Amazing how the formula is working in the background, isn't it?" I asked. "However, actually articulating the exact words can take a more determined voice. The formula uses internal dialogue to drive performance.

"You are a professor. That is clear. Do you all see that both in language and clarity of purpose?" I asked. "Professors have to teach students and his goal has what, where, and when embedded, easily, into the answer: 212 students, each semester in his class. I always laugh at utter clarity examples. Runners run. Writers write. Singers sing. Haters hate." I stopped and noticed several aha! nods.

"Ontologically speaking, if I may, human existence, or the differentiating factor for us, is our ability to have and use language in very unique ways. Without the faculty of language or internal dialogue, we are responsive to our environment as a means to survive and push our genetic code down the line. Oddly, some never get out of this trap. Nevertheless, internal dialogue drives our actions. And it seems to be this structured code is always there in every human." I paused, hoping for another bullet to kill the formula.

A lady in the front row laughed and raised her hand, "Thom, have you ever heard of neural linguistics?"

"Yes, but I am sure not to the nth degree you know of it," I said, chuckling.

"Neural linguistic program, NLP, is the theory that words spoken over time retrain the nervous system to adapt to what is being said," she explained.

"Clearly, words are powerful, and our system responds accordingly. However, NLP in general is a double-edged sword. You can tell yourself anything for a long time and you will eventually believe it . . . and so will your body. If you say you are beaten, you will be. If you say you have a chance, you will find one. I suggest NLP is a snapshot or a narrow view of the underlying formula I believe we are all born with that is encoded into our being," I said frankly, because I had studied numerous books on NLP over my lifetime.

"Let me demonstrate another aspect of the formula. I call this the paradigm of performance. What I mean by that is we all tend to only use two or three of the line items and without the linear progression of using it one through six, humans damage themselves. For instance, the diet craze that each and everyone is sucked into.

"Ma'am, why can we not lose weight and keep it off?" I redirected to the woman.

She hesitated.

"Hey, ma'am, I am not claiming to be a doctor or a dietician or a workout guru. I just know without fail, unless people change the actual language of who they say they are, they will just repeat or eventually get back to what the dialogue is telling them who they are. Losing weight is simple. Take in less than you expend. There are many ways to expend calories and many different ways to take in calories. The diet isn't the issue, although it is lucrative to never solve the weight issue. The workout isn't the issue either.

"Three very profound issues arise in this conversation about losing weight that are important. The first issue is that maybe, I mean maybe, only 20 percent of the people alive on the planet can honor their word and never give up on honoring their word. I have trained thousands to learn the process of honoring your word just for 21 days and only 20 percent can do it the first time. People give little value to their word or value making a promise and keeping it for any extended period of time," I said, fully expecting a rebuttal.

"Since those two foundational pieces to the formula are not learned or even being taught and reinforced, then the first part of the formula never even gets looked at. In effect everyone knows they need a goal and plan, line items two and five. But they never transform line item one. In effect they keep saying they are fat or out of shape or not healthy. I can tell you no plan and no goal will ever overcome a statement declaring yourself fat. Constant conflict with who you are and what you do is a terrible emotionally destructive way to live.

"Yet when that person kills off the fat dialogue first and replaces it with I am fit or I am sexy or I am a runner, what immediately becomes available to them? Right in that moment?" I slowed my voice down and paused.

The woman said, "Anything becomes possible. But they don't immediately lose weight, that is for sure."

"Yeah, humans—even while looking at what is possible—kill it off so quickly . . . just like you did. Because it is rare people allow themselves to master who they are first. Because if you knew who you were and really honored it, what would you do?"

She said, "I would do the things that aligned with who I thought I was, and I would surround myself with people who supported me!"

I smiled. "No argument at all. And everyone alive is doing just that. Everyone does the things that align with who they are, and everyone gets a support group to support those activities. That is the formula running in the background. Yet few of us use internal dialogue or take ownership of our statement of who we are as the first step to growth. We instead allow what we do and what we look like and what we are dealing with tell us 'who' we are. A rather desperate condition!"

Many existential conversations happened over the course of the three-hour discussion. A deeper dive into NLP fascinated me to the level at which the concept was known and being explored in academia and being used to various degrees of success across what I call the five pyramids of human performance. Many direct inquiries into post-traumatic stress (PTS) and explosive-related brain injuries shocked me. I had to admit I have no direct experience with either, which I noticed shocked them more. Eventually, I paused a heated debate between several doctors and the chair of the meeting regarding the effects of PTS and brain injuries on decision-making skills:

"My friends, I witnessed many killings and many deaths of both the enemy and my brothers and sisters. I felt the explosive waves of more than 50 explosions within 50 feet of my body. In one firefight, I got hit twice in the body armor chest plate and somehow received two bullet holes through the crotch of my pants. Maybe all that stuff affected my conscious and subconscious decision-making skills and even my abilities," I said, standing up to merely make a point.

"You all surely see the terribly mangled and affected men and women from war; some can barely breathe, hardly talk, or scarcely move at all without pain and help. War takes a toll on the ones directly in the battle, it indirectly impacts their families, and until now, I didn't realize that it also changes the science of the mind. War is neither good nor bad. War will exist for every generation until the human species is completely gone. That is the way of life.

"I am keenly interested in human beings or, rather, the being side of humans. Not too particularly interested in what people do. That may seem odd to you. Maybe that is not, because you all know actions are the end result of a ton of things, thoughts, and experiences that manifest in the action witnessed. I am looking for the origin of the action," I said, simply saying what was true for me.

"This magnificent internal dialogue, or as you say it, this ability to use language to program actions excites me. To speak the world into existence has a particular format and formula that seems to be present with everyone. Either by commission or omission, the formula gets coded and the actions and outcomes become very predictable. I am asking you to help me explain the formula or help me destroy it because it doesn't work. As I stand here, I only see it working perfectly in everyone in the audience." I walked slowly back to my chair. That warrior part of me felt the hair on the back of my neck rise. The urge to run or turn and fight was almost overwhelming.

Upon sitting, I felt out of place, like I had just turned over a cart of food into a puddle when everyone was hungry. The chairman looked at me and suggested a 15-minute break to refresh and discuss the final conversation with the attending professionals. I took it as a cue to run like I was being chased, but I simply went to the restroom and to get a cup of coffee.

The sudden drop I had experienced both from failing out of West Point and out of SEAL training so many times again electrified my senses, and the world slowed down. The similar experience of combat when bullets started flying and everything slowed down and I could speed up and feel everything is quite intoxicating. For 15 minutes everything was clear and detailed and made sense.

As I waited outside the room for the next steps, my sense of smell could detect stress and an edgy presentation from the room. My wife hates my sense of smell because she cannot hide from it, nor can the kids. When the door opened and the chairman came out, he was smiling. "Thom, do you have time to present the whole formula and answer questions about it?" he asked as he came toward me.

"I have time, but the formula explanation cannot be done in the abstract. I have to have five people to ask questions, people who are open enough to answer," I said. I doubted doctors would expose themselves to real questions anyway.

"Yes," he quickly replied. "I want to see you turn on your warrior mind and do it, like you and I engaged last month."

The chairman began with his story of our one-day training. Although we had spent an entire day diving into what he called "the bowels" of the human mind, I do not recall the particulars of the discussion. For me the day was merely a brief discussion of leading men in combat and what it had been like to kill and witness killing. I had mentioned the formula for human performance and asked him questions and used the questions to fill in the six parts of the formula. The experience had seemed insignificant yet had impacted him greatly.

"Thom and I spent a day together discussing the impact of war on him. I had originally wanted to speak with Thom because I had read his book *Unbreakable: A Navy SEAL's Way of Life*. His stories were remarkable, then we arrived at the point of the discussion where he brought forward the formula that he suggests is present in everyone. What I found particularly interesting was the part that suggests the formula can be coded and recoded and human actions change accordingly." Pausing, he looked at me.

"We spent one hour discussing how I code my physical formula using particular language structures and how I select people to support me. I walked away both excited and disturbed," he said, looking at me again as I smiled and shrugged. "I have asked him to conduct a question and answer with five of you to determine if the formula works and can be coded."

At this particular point in the discussion, our discussion between you and me, I want to pause a moment. The older I become, the less I hide from the truth or, rather, imperfections. When I was young imperfections were never to be exposed, because someone would discover I shouldn't be here or point out I may not be able to lead or win. Throughout a career of training to expose imperfections and then sharpening them so that they were not so imperfect, I came to realize humans have flaws . . . a lot of flaws. Ironically, knowing you have flaws and imperfections and exposing them to cure them or exposing them to realize you have to prevent them from surfacing at the wrong time was the mastery of the SEAL teams in combat.

I once again knew I had to expose the flaws and cover up some of the imperfections at this juncture in the discussion. As you read, know that I selected to not expose one particular flaw in the formula, one that I had a hard time reconciling. The flaw that I still cannot reconcile is that the formula can be used to both destroy and build the human condition. The eternal battle with dark and light.

With that, five people who wanted to go through the exercise of filling in a particular formula were identified. And we began a four-hour marathon into internal dialogue and the formula for human performance.

"Let me begin with a particular statement that captures internal dialogue and coding the formula. I do not know who said it first and wish I could acknowledge them for saying it. The saying goes like this: 'Who you say you are gives you access to living that life. But you must commit to simple actions every day to climb out of the mud.' I had heard this many times in my life but had focused on the wrong aspect of that saying. I had focused on the premise you can work your way out of a bad situation. That is true to a point," I said, pausing to get a drink.

"The point of failure is subtle at first but very clear and poignant now. That point is when who you say you *are* is counter to what you *do*. Because your actions in the short run will never overpower who you say you are in the long run. So today's questions and answers are my attempt to align who you say you are with actions for you to take to arrive at who you are in a measurable way." I smiled and stopped.

I then reengaged. "If you all allow me to begin with the physical pyramid first, if only for the reason that most concepts are easier to realize in a visceral setting. And, trust me, the physical pyramid is very visceral." With that, the woman who had self-selected to work on her particular formula came to the stage and we began.

"Who are you physically? That is the first in order of value and often is the hardest question to answer. It is hard to answer because no one is taught to look at who they are being," I said.

"I want to be healthy and fit," she replied.

My heart sank as she answered with the common reflection on how we look at ourselves. I always find it odd that people answer a simple question with an emotional plea for help. First of all, you cannot *be* who you want to be. You can only *be* who you are being. Turning to the woman, I tried a different tack: "Try answering that simple question with who you are actually being right now."

"Well, I am fit, then," she answered.

I looked at her and at the audience and realized I would have to smooth this out if I had any hopes of not offending. "Wanting something you do not have is powerful. It is an emotion called desire. Using emotions is line item three in the formula. It is a statement of need that draws on the power of emotions as a tool to achieve success. We will get to that. But line item three is line item three and, trust me, isn't very useful when you cannot capture line item one. So who are you being right now? Who is the person you are, physically, right now?" I walked over and stood right in front of her as I asked the question.

"I want to be fit; what is wrong with wanting to be a better version of myself?" she asked very matter-of-factly.

"It is a trap to try to be something you are not. It is not sustainable. You will eventually only arrive at the person you say you are. I don't mean to be esoteric with that statement. God knows I am not esoteric. The vicious cycle of doing things that are not in alignment with who you are is hard to watch. Diets to lose weight because you don't like who you are always implode, and the fat person wins out. Lifting weights to feed the vanity of looking better always succumbs to the mirror telling you that you look one way or the other. We are all caught up in the cycle. Just because everyone is doing it isn't powerful or even useful. And, trust me, it is very expensive to pay for that misalignment," I said, laughing. "Try this, use language to describe who you are right now in this moment," I said.

In that moment I saw her begin to break down. Not a bad breakdown. She realized who she was. "I am unfit," she answered. "I am fat," she acknowledged.

"Yes, you are fat. And you do things and surround yourself with people who support that way of being. That is brilliant. You see that as wrong. I see that as powerful beyond measure. Why do you see that as a bad thing?" I asked.

"I don't want to be fat," she said.

"That is not how life works. I can tell you that is not the way the formula that you were born with is working. You can fight it, but you will lose. And you are losing the desire battle because you are not using desire in the correct sequence. What is winning is being fat or unfit," I said. "What you don't know is that you can recode or change the language of the formula. You can change it without evidence. Changing the declaration of who you are immediately rewrites the entire formula," I said. "The reality is you don't have to embrace fat or fit or resign yourself to a way of being and a way of life. The formula needs only to be coded, and it will cause actions predicate to the wording. So let's keep seeing how you now code it," I suggested. "What is your current measurable goal?"

Goals are always a struggle for people out of alignment. Goals are replaced with actions, or the plan and disparity of activity ensues. "My goal is to work out three times a week and to eat healthy," she stated plainly.

"No, that is the plan," I answered. "It is common to use the formula out of sequence. It is common to not understand a goal-driven life. Now who are people or partners that support you being fat?" I asked, knowing this would be eye opening.

"What do you mean who are people supporting my being fat?" she asked. "I don't think I have people supporting me being fat. I have a dietician and a trainer at the gym helping me to lose weight and get fit."

"Structurally, that is inaccurate. You are fat trying to look thin. Yes, they are trying to help you look thin, but they are really empowering who you are, which is 'I am fat.'" I smiled and tried to be nonconfrontational.

"You, and all of us, actually, were born with preexisting 'I am' dialogues. Rather, the dialogues are already encoded into the formula of human performance from the first time language shows up for human beings," I said as I walked to the white board to write the five encoded dialogues. "I apologize," I continued, "my experience validates that everyone starts out with these five at age three and many unlearn them through trauma, yet a few keep them going. If you will let me, I will write them down on the board." I picked up the pen and wrote them all in order.

1. Physical dialogue is "I Am Unbreakable"

2. Intellectual dialogue is "I Am Infinite"

3. Wealth dialogue is "I Am Abundant"

4. Relationship dialogue is "I Am One"

5. Spiritual dialogue is "I Am Connected"

"Perhaps, let me also write down the dialogues we experience in our lives due to being uninformed and often smashed by the environment we exist in," I said.

1. Physically environmentally dependent is "I Am Broken"
2. Intellectually circumstantial is "I Am Finite"
3. Wealth exclusionary is "I Am Scarce"
4. Relationship experience is "I Am Separate"
5. Spiritually delusional is "I Am Alone"

I turned and made an exaggerated stretching motion and lifted my knees and jogged in place, saying, "Oh dear, this is going to hurt. Give me a second to prepare for the beating." We all laughed at the unexpected momemt of levity.

"There are four times in every human's life where language changes them or where life shifts. If I may, I would like to bring them up then ask you if it is useful to know them and useful to the formula," I said.

"Research suggests the first time humans recognize language as a transformative tool is around age three. Obviously, speaking happens early, but transformative language occurs around three when young people ask themselves this question about themselves. And I find it ironic, given your point of view, that they ask a question regarding who they are. The question is: Is something wrong with me? All of us asked ourselves that question and spend our formative years, actually around 10 years of age, seeking that answer," I said.

"At around 10 to 13 years, we all come to another injection point of language where we have answered that question. Oddly, we all answer it the same way. The answer is: something *is* wrong with me. And for the next 10 years or so, we seek to answer that question, as well." I stopped and looked at the chairman. "Do you notice the 'being' verbs? They are very important for humans to resolve," I said, and he shook his head in acknowledgement

"Next, at between 18 and 21 years of age, we all resolve the answer to the fundamental question we are all asking. The answer always is: I don't fit in. And for the next 15 years or so, we try to prove we don't fit in to various groups or environments in life," I said, laughing.

"What is funny to me is the final injection point where language completely transforms the future or kills the future of everyone. Some call it the midlife crisis, and there is evidence to support the notion of midlife crisis as well. But we can discuss that separately at a fee," I said, and everyone laughed with me. "At 35, humans have been trying to prove they fit in or don't fit in, that one group is better, and one is worse, or that right is right and wrong is wrong. I call this injection point the crossroads of life. At this crossroads I have seen people turn 90 degrees in attitude and actions. I have also seen people not pivot and stay with proving right and wrong. The ones who pivot have a truly miraculous life. The ones who stay the course seem to have a difficult life and often hit a wall and stop living." I paused to see if they were listening or checked out. They were listening!

"The language at the crossroads is this: This is *not* me, that over there *is* me. They get tired of fighting who they are *not* and take the leap and just want to be the person they *are*. Even if they have to give up family, money, or a limb, they pivot to finally realize who they really *are*." With that, I stopped and sat down.

For a long time, it seemed I just sat there and looked into their faces. The excitement to share with professionals in the "mind space" brought me to risking sharing my experience. As the seconds ticked by, I braced for the impact of those professionals completely destroying the notion that I had regarding the formula and language being the center point of focus. In the SEAL teams, when you bring up a new idea, even if you know it will solve problems, you have to fight and beat down the older SEALs who already have a solution to everything. I mean *really* fight them. Oddly, fighting and winning means your idea gets absorbed, losing means it doesn't. So I sat there wondering if I would fight to win . . . or if I should fight.

"Thom, we agree," said a man who stood up and spoke clearly. "We all formally learned what you just discussed. You sure took a complicated process and made it less so. And you missed a great deal. Yet I agree with the premise. Now how do you use the formula and the four transformational time event?" he asked.

I laughed. "Honestly, I anticipated a fight. I use the four times language changes performance as an investigation with the person I am training to resolve the horrible performance I am witnessing. Meaning when people are not doing well in any of the five pyramids, the reason is the why in which they have used language at one of those ages to deal with demonstrative events in between the points. The formula was filled out with those words that came from those experiences, and their actions are always predicate to who they said they were. Once I find that out, I kill off the old 'I am' dialogue and help them find a new one," I said, not wanting to debate or convince.

"Everyone," I said, standing up and walking to the front of the stage, "seems to be stuck in their past events and stuck into this point of view. They have constructed language around defining who they are because of the event. If you get treated poorly at a young age by the opposite sex or by someone of another race, then you blame yourself before age 13, or you make it mean they are wrong at age 21. The more brutal the events, the more people define who they are. Meanwhile, this formula that is always running in the background, always needing to be filled in with wording of any kind, gets filled in, and the engine turns on and outcomes happen according to the dialogue we used. I know that is a simpleton's view, but that is as base level as I have been able to resolve it so that I can understand it and be able to teach it to others," I said.

"Experiences shape us—that is clear. How we process and make sense of those experiences also shapes every one of us. Yet what I have noticed is the 'I am' statement can be reset. Reset by experiences and reset simply by resetting. I know as a matter of fact who people say they are is the starting point of all actions and outcomes. Sadly, who they say they are now happens during those four times in life instead of each day," I said.

A stunning woman in the middle of the room stood up and said, "Thom, we agree. You are on to something, but that information is old. I want to use the relationship formula. Can you help me fill in mine?" she asked as she walked forward.

Apparently, I could not say no.

"I would only ask this of you," I said as we shook hands and she sat down facing the whiteboard. "I ask you to not add drama as to why your relationship is failing if it is or try to convince me you are being treated poorly by him. Okay?" She acknowledged and we continued.

"First, your declaration statement is: 'I am one with,'" I turned and looked at her, waiting for his name, "Jon. By the way, that is true, do you understand that up front? Do you get that you are one with everyone and especially Jon?

"Second, and always the hardest goal to capture in all the five pyramids, is how do you define a relationship goal? The goal needs the answer what the metric is, when the thing is going to happen, and where the thing is going to happen. Normally this would take hours for a person in a relationship to define. If you will let me, I will accelerate the filling out of the goal." I stopped to get her agreement.

"Measuring a relationship isn't hard, but it isn't how much you love or feel for the other person. Love cannot be measured, and feelings are often not measurable, since few can control feelings at all. And I point out that feelings are line item three, not line item two. So if you are going to relate to another person, how do you measure that relationship? First, you have to actually have three of your own goals. You have to have a physical goal, an intellectual goal, and a wealth goal. If you don't have those, you cannot be in relationship. You can have passion and sex, but not be in a relationship." I stopped and let that sink in.

"Second, your partner has to have their three goals clearly defined. This is the hardest aspect of relationship work. So few people have goals, and fewer still allow and even know what their partner's goals are. So what are your partner's three goals?" I lifted the pen to write on the white board, knowing she would not know them.

"Interesting, Jon likes to hike, he is trying to figure out how to hire a contractor, and he owns a manufacturing business," she said, surprising me with her answser.

"Okay, just so you know, 'likes to hike' is not a measurable goal, nor are the other two you referenced. But I am excited you know that much about your spouse. Few partners know very much about each other outside of their emotions and problems. So what are Jon's defined goals?" I pushed back.

"I don't know them exactly," she answered.

"So let's try it this way. Let's you and I have a relationship right now! My physical goal is to complete a 100-mile ultramarathon in September in Utah. My intellectual is to learn about neural linguistic programming by June in California. My wealth goal is to have 10 clients in the program in South Carolina by October. Now those are my goals. What are yours?" I drew a line down the middle of the white board separating my goals on the right from the space for her goals on the left. She shared her three goals with me, and I wrote them down.

"Now we are in a very profound relationship. I know who you are and what your goals are. We are in the top 20 percent of all the people alive because we have clarity regarding the other person. Did that take time or drama?" I asked. She said no. "So here is the reality of filling in the relationship formula . . . you don't get a choice of what your partner's goals are. You cannot change them or manipulate them in any way. People are going to do what they are going to do with or without you. Once you have expressed clarity with each other, you can then decide to support with 100 percent of yourself, which I will tell you is the only way to go. Or you can leave, which is also very powerful. The worst thing you can do is stay in an unsupportive relationship, one which you don't try to help them achieve their goals. Personally, I think this is why so many people get divorced and so many leaders fail," I said.

"A show of hands, how many in the audience have three defined personal goals and have written down your partner's three goals?" I asked, anticipating 20 percent. When no one raised his or her hands, I laughed. "So you are in a relationship of convenience or sex or just to raise a family? By the way, a family goal is a wealth goal for the partner actually staying home to raise the kids," I said.

"What would your relationship be like if you knew who your partner was and what the three goals were?" I asked, because the answer is always breathtaking.

The woman on stage answered: "Fulfilling," she said.

"What stops you from having a fulfilling relationship is twofold and very uniquely tied to the four points we discussed. During those periods of time in between the four points, where bad freaking things happened, you and your partner defined who you were and what was possible. The more demonstrative and the more set in stone they become, then the possible goals and more cemented the 'I am' statement become as well. The phenomenon of distinctions leaves no room for growth and for sharing, for possibility," I said.

"The rigid life of no possibility gets to age 35, and all of a sudden you change the language of who you are. You are no longer broken as a declaration statement because you broke your leg at 10 or 17 years old. You are no longer stupid or finite because you failed a class at whatever age. You are no longer scarce or poor or useless because you are a different color or parents were mean or poor or abusive. You redefine your life, your actions change . . . as do your partners.

"All that is going on is the formula running its program in your life. Either you fill it in with determination and clarity, or the experiences you have and the environment in which you live will do it for you. The formula doesn't care how it gets filled in; it just does what it is told to do. And it always works."

The woman I had been interacting with then asked me the most important question of mentorship possible. "I admit when I was first married, my husband and I did know those three things about each other. Time goes by and we didn't grow apart, we just began to follow different interests. My question is, whom do you suggest as a teacher or mentor when changes are needed?" she asked without seeming the least bit confrontational.

"I am not a relationship coach or marriage counselor. To just focus on a relationship or marriage in isolation seems folly. I can only share what I have encountered with successful men and women and leaders when asked to measure or engage in their primary relationships. My experience shows me love and feelings alone, as a point of focus in how to deal with relationships, will destroy the relationship over time. Feelings are very reactive, and feelings and emotions are not practiced and learned skills. More importantly, asking a client to know their spouse and what their goals are is tangible and can be done quickly. Finding something tangible to relate to in the spouse or lover is the foundation of a relationship," I said.

"How many clients knew the answers when you asked them?" she asked.

"None! Not one out of 120. I want that to sink in," I said, making a point of clarity. "The fact that not one of them knew the answers shocked me. Not knowing your partner, not knowing their goals, literally disturbs your health and theirs; it diminishes their interest in learning new things; and it destroys the constructs of growing wealth. Not having a measurable way to relate to each other creates an environment such that no matter how much money you make or how much you work out or how much you read, something is draining away that you cannot explain. It's like filling a bucket with water, and every time you look in the bucket, there is less water than you put in it." Again, I paused.

"Let me skip to the end, because if I go into detail and dramatize the reasons, I think we will all be dumber. What is remarkable is what happened as each client engaged in those questions with their spouse or lover. Three crossroads immediately became available. The one, which I will discuss briefly, is when a client says, 'I don't find it valuable to know those answers. We get along okay. She or he does their own thing and I do mine.' When this is the response, I simply tell them, our training stops here because no matter what we do from here forward, there will be a drain in your time and energy which we cannot address," I said.

"The second crossroad is when they are able to write down the answers. The client immediately begins to achieve results in the three pyramids of his or her own life. They are no longer stuck. Their businesses start making progress. Their ability to accomplish physical goals, even ultramarathons, was so rapid, I was shocked. As a mentor, the experience reminds me of fluid nonconflicting action.

"However, the third crossroad happens most often. Women leaders actually want to share their goals with their spouses but have had to hide them due to some odd cultural incongruence. And the male spouse has learned to not ask due to the same cultural issues. Giving them permission is extraordinary. Helping them drop their guard, as a mentor, is very hard because the drama and sensitivity of the culture of strong women causes emotions to flare," I said, pausing because many of the women in the audience were laughing.

"What the men experience dropped me to my knees. The wives of many successful men no longer could articulate a goal for themselves in the three pyramids. Once the kids were raised and in college, the wife was lost. She had identified who she was as a function of her kids for so long, she could not reset the declaration statement. And her personals goals were artificially misaligned with actions or the plan or line item five. Goals are not activities or actions; meaning going to the gym and working out without a defined goal is where most wives found themselves. Also, reading or watching TV as a means to escape isn't learning. Harder still was to witness the wives who could not define any measurement of value or wealth," I said.

"The process to recapture a lost relationship, I mean one that doesn't have clarity of the other person's goals, was exhausting to me. A fundamental truth became clear. When you are one with your lover or spouse, you don't get to decide on their goals. You only get to support them. No matter what! And the effort to accomplish unwavering support was like pulling teeth from a grizzly bear," I said, laughing with the audience. "Relationships are all in or just leave. That is the truth! If you cannot share your goals and have your partner share their goals, you are causing more damage than you could possibly imagine." I walked to the woman on stage and looked at her.

For the rest of the question and answer session, I asked questions instead of answering them. I wanted to know solutions to get successful couples to engage in meaningful ways with each other. Finding the simple actions in the midst of the complexities of emotions and relationship dynamics remains my commitment to this very day. I wanted to know how to solve the time and energy equation of relationships. Without satisfying that equation I knew working with clients who want to continue upward growth in all five pyramids would reach a barrier.

Carving out the foundation of honoring your word and never giving up takes four weeks. In four weeks, the time and energy used literally recodes your DNA. Carving out the first vertical growth component occurred to me during the last hour of the event with professional psychologists and psychiatrists. The time commitment is slight; the energy spent depends solely on one's ability to not react emotionally. Simple, but not easy!

Three simple things in relationship only take 30 minutes a day. Every single day for the rest of your life to build a strong foundation, you must listen to your partner's goals, you must share your goals, then you must touch or create intimacy. Each of the three as a baseline only requires 10 minutes in each phase.

The Method: The six-part human performance formula to produce a measurable life in five areas works every time you use it. Declare who you are, have a huge goal, meet your needs, have six people committed to helping you, make a plan to execute three simple things a day, and have a simple answer to why.

    1. Declare

    2. Goal

    3. Needs

    4. Partners

    5. Plan

    6. Why

CHAPTER FOUR

Three Simple Things

The Process: Find the simple in all the complexity of chaos. Set up the five nonnegotiable baselines. The structure of the three simple things is the same for each of the five pyramids.

How do you build and sustain foundations for success over time? It sounds simple, but again, it isn't. You must organize six hours of your day around three simple things for each of the five pyramids (spiritual, relationship, intellectual, wealth building, and physical), and to build a solid foundation, you must do it consistently for 21 days. If you stumble, start over. Don't let emotions control your outcomes. By the time you reach the end of this chapter, you will have learned how to set up three nonnegotiable activities for each of the five pyramids of success. Remember that nothing grows at a steady upward rate. All growth for humans is like the sun rising in the morning and setting at night. Growth is meant to be up and down.

1. Offense actions and words and time demands

2. Defense actions and words and time demands

3. Strategic actions and words and time demands

Each of the five pyramids I outline in this book will have distinct actions and words to reflect three simple things. Each will also require different time demands that are nonnegotiable. These three simple things become the baseline activities you do each day in order to sustain performance in your life, no matter what level of success you have attained.

Imagine if you have arrived at the state of performance where you have proven to yourself you can honor your word and have overcome your excuses for 21 days straight? Consider, then, the real-world implications of having faced a particular fear and overcoming that fear through actions. Finally, revel in the fact you have pushed through your own self-imposed limits by moving for 24 hours.

Scary to imagine because you would have a level of power in this world few can even consider. You created the foundation to "speak the world into existence" and resisted the excuses long enough to see the whisper become real.

The gift for all human beings is to create that foundation for themselves through those three trials. For me, I am honored to be a facilitator for 85 human beings, creating that foundation through the initial process described.

The type of foundation for your life and next steps the three trials establish are solid. And even if the foundation cracks and slips, all that is needed is to make a new promise and keep it, move toward what you are afraid of, and push through your self-imposed limits again for 24 hours. The process is simple, but not easy. What then can you or, rather, are you *willing* to build on that foundation? More importantly, what will be built that can be sustained over time?

Before we get deep into the method to sustain what is built, I will share several truths. Clearly, everyone wants to be number one; apparently, every business and sales presentation wants to claim upward growth indefinitely; and, honestly, most athletes want to get stronger and faster and go longer and longer.

The reality that exists in the world is none of that is sustainable over time. Nothing that has ever been created constantly grows on an upward chart graph. That is the lie that is being sold everywhere. So this lie we tell ourselves isn't what I will show you to build on the foundation of honoring your word, facing your fears, and pushing your limits.

What I suggest being far more powerful is to build a way of engaging your life, wherever you are, on the up or down curve. Build on this strong foundation a method to engage three simple things. By having the foundation and building from it five areas of life where your baseline engagement is to simply do three simple things is powerful and sustainable. The second method in the process to set up a nonnegotiable six-hour day is to craft three simple things in each of the five pyramids of your life.

I have to admit, in all the training of leaders or top athletes, and even in Navy SEAL training, the sheer commitment required to break through the complexity of what it takes to be successful and pulling out three simple basic things may be the differentiating factor in success. Consider the simplicity, yet recognize the effort is not easy. The process is impossible if you quit. The process is impossible when you are afraid to take action. The process to get to three simple things cannot be completed if you cannot endure the 24-hour challenge.

The attrition rate of 85 percent in SEAL training is because the ones who quit cannot do simple things. Quitters make life complex. Quitters quit out of fear, and fear makes you not capable of doing simple things. Quitters cannot endure the strain of dealing with their own demons for 24 hours. Yet if you have read the above trials, and in reading the words you actually went forward and completed the trials, you are ready to sift through the complexity of your life and find the simple.

Finding Simple in the Complex

I really like shooting rifles. Before the SEAL teams I shot rifles, shotguns, pistols, BB guns, bow and arrows, and slingshots. The true enjoyment of shooting took me into the woods everywhere in North America. With no money to get expensive guns or pay for high-end hunts, I had to keep things simple . . . and oftentimes sneaky. I probably hunted on private land more times than I should have, but when you are hundreds of miles from any paved roads and there are no signs, passion takes over.

Yet shooting is simple. To the untrained person, shooting is complex and dangerous and scary and may be equivalent to the worst nightmare you never wanted to have. Shooting is simple when the shooter processes the complexity into three simple things.

The foundation is built exactly the same:

- Shoot every day for 21 days.

- Overcome the fear of weapons by learning and handling them.

- Shoot or hunt for 24 hours.

What you establish as a foundation is that you as the shooter are just the platform. The platform is merely to always hold the rifle, pistol, or bow the same. Period! The unbearable boringness of consistency! Without consistency, 200 yards is the limit. With consistency, 1,500 yards is rather simple. The three simple things in shooting are to sight the picture, squeeze, and follow through.

Man, anyone can do that! Anyone *can*, you are correct! But few actually do.

It takes a SEAL going through sniper training 12 weeks to sift through the complexity and just do three simple things. And many fail out because they cannot apply the three fundamental aspects of shooting in all conditions. Shooting, like everything in life that you want to do, immediately feels odd at first. Running feels odd. Studying feels odd. New presentations feel odd. All new events, new situations, new *anything* feels odd.

The first time you pick up a rifle, your senses are overwhelmed with everything. The weight is new. The feel and texture are new. Add what people may have mistakenly told you about rifles, with emotions that you may harbor and the fear you may add to the experience, and that makes it more complex. The sound of a rifle going off actually hurts your eardrums and your shoulder, and pain makes all things complex. The jump of the rifle when it goes off is odd. All very complex!

Emotions are not one of the three simple things, clearly. Real shooters aren't emotional. For instance, if you have ever heard of "buck fever," then you know that someone with buck fever isn't dealing with just three things. I have seen men get emotional buck fever when a deer walks out, and they cycle their bolt five times without shooting a round. Then they ask, "Did I get him?" More to the point, three simple things of sight picture, squeeze, and follow through are nonnegotiable and need to be the baseline a shooter does every single time. Emotion destroys effectiveness, to be sure. Emotion adds complexity.

We all carry so much baggage, so much emotional commitment to past circumstances, that breaking through all that complexity the emotion and baggage add takes time. The shooting analogy is poignant. Just holding the rifle the same way no matter what was the shooting condition that drove most of my sniper instructors crazy. "Knees out, heels down, for God's sake," they would say for weeks. "Stop taking your cheek off the gun between shots" would be another fun reminder. "You slapped the trigger; the gun goes off when it goes off! Don't be in a hurry" was my favorite reminder.

Yet all these demonstrations, all the constant coaching to make three simple things the only things the snipers focused on, is the necessary evil of making a sniper. Don't think, don't do it your way, don't do it the way Daddy taught you, and especially don't do it the way some movie portrayed. Do it the same way every time and practice doing it the same way every time for 10,000 shots. I have found no other way to teach and ingrain the art and science of sniping into the shooter but to teach simplicity and repetition.

The method of three simple things practiced constantly is boring. Boring is unbearable because it is not flashy or cool, nor is it new branding for the new you. Practice the method until there is no other way, until three simple things are injected into your DNA and get passed on to your child like hair color. This method of three simple things is the *only* way.

Spiritual Baseline: Three Simple Things

There are two times of day to engage your spiritual baseline. During the 21-day challenge to honor your word and never give up, you learned to carve out the simple time and simple activities needed to succeed. The purpose of the challenge was to create both a foundation for growth and to initialize the method to produce three simple things in your spiritual life.

The first 15 minutes in the morning and the last 15 minutes at night are the two vital times to define who you are. There is nothing esoteric about spiritual time and spiritual actions. Few spend any concentrated time acquiring spiritual connections. These two times are crucial to intentionally programming your being through a process. Most skip these two times and are instead being programmed by their environments or by stressors.

In point of fact, your body is a temple for all of your experiences to come together and have meaning. Your five senses are conduits to interpret the challenges of your life that day. Finally, your ability to evoke and measure the five pyramids of human performance by acts of prayer or meditation profoundly give you access to taking intentional actions to deliver the results you want. Carve out the 30 minutes of spiritual growth every day and make them nonnegotiable. Period.

1. (Offense) Wake up and immediately move every muscle and joint in your body.

2. (Defense) Engage and turn on each of your five senses.

3. (Strategic) Read each of your five formulas out loud.

Relationship Baseline: Three Simple Things

Much personal research and experience gained through training both men and women to acquire a baseline shows there are two times during the day to create and establish and maintain relationships. Through many failures on my part, I now put all my effort to make clear how vital relationship success is by telling my mentees to engage with their key relationships immediately after conducting their spiritual awakening in the morning. Then, at night, I tell them to go through that process again. The key relationships you have at home with your wife, your husband, and/or your kids determine the impact and influence you have with all the people in your life and the extent to which you succeed in all the other pyramids. No man or woman can exist for any period of time at a high level of performance without a keen awareness of the value of what happens at home.

Relationships are inherently complex. The deeper the commitment, the bigger the family, the more complexities arise. Emotional involvement, which is a common reaction to the complexities of having another human being in your life, adds a level of complexity that many cannot deal with. Yet a relationship intentionally left unaddressed will cause the demise of health and wealth eventually.

The predictable divorce of a leader who works a 12-hour day clearly reduces all the business or wealth successes to half. As does the lack of attention leading up to the divorce cause the loss of energy and support. Unintentional relationship work is the predictable downfall of many leaders and high functioning winners.

The three simple things in relationship change everything, yet it is very difficult to carve out both the time and actions needed. Each day only takes 30 minutes of time to achieve the baseline. And if you don't give 30 minutes, your partner will demand three hours!

1. (Offense) Listen to your partner's goals and what they are doing that day.

2. (Defense) Speak of your goals and articulate what you will do that day.

3. (Strategic) Touch each other and be intimate.

Simple, but not easy! From what I have seen, this is the hardest challenge for most . . . to carve out time and actually do the three activities. I hear every possible excuse and reason imaginable not to do them; obviously, this is the hardest aspect of being in a successful relationship. So many excuses from people exist in a profound relationship who cannot do three simple things. The herculean effort is worth it!

My effort to encourage clients to accomplish these three simple things admittedly is the most difficult drama-filled aspect of training. Spending 30 minutes a day as if the task is nonnegotiable will create so much momentum and support and enthusiasm in your key relationships, your life will never be stale again. Use the process of honoring your word, never giving up and establishing your baseline. Literally: Do the three simple things every day for 21 days straight. Don't excuse yourself! Distance, travel, or being tired or not in the mood are worthless excuses. That your partner yelled at you doesn't cut it. Do it *anyway*. Say what you are afraid to say! Don't separate yourself from them for any cultural notion. Get to it and don't look back.

Physical Baseline: Three Simple Things

Let's pause here just one moment. Imagine we are sitting around a fire and having a nondefensive chat about our bodies, our health, and what you have done physically in your life. Here is the secret: Your body gave you exactly what you asked of it. Truth is never good or bad! As you sit and come to terms with your body and health and let that reality sink in, you will laugh.

Some men and women can run and push themselves physically and mentally for hundreds of miles. Many can go days without sleep. Many can get blown up and then make their way to an aid station. Others cannot get off the couch or drink themselves to death. Some commit suicide. None of that is good or bad: It is just a testament to this wonderful body you have and what it will do for you when and if you ask it to deliver. Your body is a temple and reflects what you put into it in order to get something out of it.

I have not only asked my body to do things I never thought were possible, but I've also trained hundreds of men and women to take complete ownership of their body and mentored them through the process to use language to produce a reality they never thought possible. The body can go from couch potato to ultramarathon runner in six months just by doing three simple things. The body can go from hypertension and pre-diabetic to healthy and fit in three months as well.

For me, the physical pyramid is the most nonnegotiable because the body goes with you everywhere, and when you are clear as to what you are asking of it, then you add an unneeded complexity to every single other pyramid. When you are on point and intentional, you literally cut through other complexities and can endure a great deal.

The time of day when you engage your physical goals is not as critical as when you engage with spiritual and relationship. Most successful men and women engage their primary activity in the morning, then later in the day, engage their secondary. Most professional athletes engage midday. Several young men and women engage in the activities after school. In some instances, many people engage these prescribed activities at night after their families go to bed. Point being, when you choose to engage the three activities is not critical, yet remains a nonnegotiable part of every day.

1. (Offense) One hour of specific activity related to your goal

2. (Defense) Twenty minutes of on point stretching

3. (Strategic) Ten glasses of water

Ninety minutes a day for the rest of your life. Do it! Stop negotiating with the one thing you can control that demonstratively impacts everything you do. You can control how you feel and your emotions by being on point with your health. You can control anxiety and patience the moment you stop talking yourself out of your 90 minutes of health, every single day. You will endure stresses at work, you will look fit and sexy and won't need a hack or surgery, and you will be able to do extraordinary things when your grandchildren ask you to.

Wealth Baseline: Three Simple Things

The baseline time required to be successful in all wealth pursuits is three hours. Three hours of highly focused, on-point activity. The stray voltage, the sporadic activity, the long enduring meetings that lead to a 12- or 14-hour day are all caused by neglecting the baseline of wealth. Time itself as a metric of efficiency and effectiveness is the most destructive way to produce wealth.

An 8-hour workday, or a 40-hour workweek as a means to represent building wealth or paying for service may be the most crippling way to producing wealth and in turn measuring value. A boss working 14-hour days six days a week for 10 years clearly is the norm, but it's not the path to being successful. Filling the wealth equation with time makes everyone lazy, both in his or her mind and actions.

1. (Offense) One hour pursuing new business

2. (Defense) One hour maturing existing business

3. (Strategic) One hour thinking and doing activity that is unconstrained by existing circumstances

These three distinct and separate activities with different thought processes as a baseline will launch you or your business to levels that cannot be attained by the old 14-hour-day paradigm. Historically, most leaders find themselves spending an inordinate amount of time just doing defensive business. Nurturing and maintaining existing clients is important and comfortable. Many years can go by without incident by just taking care of existing clients. Defensive operations are comfortable and predictable. My experience shows me that most organizations and leaders spend 85 percent of their day dealing with existing clients.

Prospecting and pursuing new business is the most uncomfortable experience to witness as a trainer and consultant. The effort for many is so disheartening that they literally stop doing it once their perceived wealth has hit a particular level. We researched several businesses and found very little concentrated effort is put into finding and engaging new clients. The fact is, everyone in the organization is responsible for finding new clients. This effort cannot be compartmentalized to sales and marketing.

Meanwhile, the final hour of unconstrained, unrestricted thoughts and actions wins the success game in the long run. One hour attempting to think out of the box or lay out a plan to arrive at some new wealth goal in two or five years is the effort of winners and is neglected by losers. Strategic thinking is hard because the future can rarely be pinned down. Our thoughts and actions are always being constrained by circumstances and uncontrollable events. Yet this hour is nonnegotiable for everyone.

Let your mind think big. Let it have time to dream and begin to plan the steps to climb into areas that threaten it. Flex this strategic muscle every single day.

Intellectual Baseline: Three Simple Things

The question isn't "Are you smart?" The statement regarding who you are intellectually is that you learn and apply what you learn to your life. Not only does your mind have the capacity to acquire information, but you—as an entire system, from muscles to actions—are functionally designed to *want* to learn.

1. (Offense) Ten minutes a day learning something that you know you don't know; (Defense) Ten minutes a day learning something that you already know; (Strategic) Ten minutes a day learning something that you didn't know you *didn't* know!

There is infinite knowledge in the universe. Give yourself the advantage of realizing that truth and spending time each day learning three simple things. Great leaders at some point in life come to realize they don't know everything. Arriving at that mental state is the key to accessing real success. You must consume new information. Seek to learn something you don't know . . . or something you know very little about. As a baseline, allow yourself 10 minutes every day to learn something new or a different way to approach something that has become rote.

The baseline 10 minutes of defensive thinking is important for a master craftsman. I call this honing your skills and getting better at what you have already developed as a strong suit. Keep learning and correcting and making better the things you already do well.

The final 10 minutes will be a unique test in acquiring knowledge. Commit to spending 10 minutes discovering ideas about things you never knew that you never knew about. Allow for epiphanies, insights, and aha moments. Most people completely disregard that area in life where they look at answering the fundamental question: "What am I missing that would make a difference?" Open your mind to what you are missing and what you have not considered.

The Method: Six-hour on-point day.

1. Spiritual baseline: 30 minutes

2. Relationship baseline: 30 minutes

3. Physical baseline: 90 minutes

4. Wealth baseline: Three hours

5. Intellectual baseline: 30 minutes

CHAPTER FIVE

Determine the Baseline

*The Process: Establishing the baseline of time and energy
expended in sequential priority makes growth sustainable.*

There's a hack for everything. Stop using hacks! There is no quick and easy way of getting things done that is sustainable. Stop searching for shortcuts! Unfortunately, there are no hacks for mastering the five pyramids. You must learn them sequentially. I learned this the hard way and I don't want you to. While it may be tempting to go directly to the wealth building pyramid to hack the system, it won't work over time, I assure you. Without the fundamentals, nothing else works. This is true in businesses too. Companies are not unlike people, and in this chapter, I'll give you a look at how the pyramids work in a business setting to prove that you cannot hack the system, no matter how tempting it is to try. You must train over and over on the basics.

Sequential Learning

While being trained by masters in each of the five pyramids of human performance separately, my goal turned toward combining all five into one distinct process in order to teach others. My initial attempt failed miserably. The failure was in not realizing there was a sequence, or level of priority, to learning the five pyramids. The effect was brutal on the client. The training actually caused more damage out of sequence than had we done nothing at all.

My analogy to learning the five pyramids out of sequence is like looking down a rifle barrel to see if the gun is loaded while pulling the trigger. Yeah, the gun is loaded and seems to work rather well, but half of your face is gone. No one wants to have that effect, yet I had literally shot my client in the face.

My initial goal was to teach clients wealth. Honestly, I also succumbed to the demand from clients to make more money. Everyone seems to want money and grow a business and all that money seems to represent. I was wrong, dangerously wrong. What was worse is that the out-of-sequence process immediately caused problems and loss of money and organizational growth.

The Pursuit of Wealth First Will Destroy You!

Let me first define our notion of wealth. Wealth is the compensation for the measurable value you provide. Seeing the process make wealth decrease so quickly made me question what my mentors taught me, and clearly, I lost the contract. Many long, heated conversations with my millionaire mentors ensued. Had I been in the SEAL teams and someone taught me something so grossly wrong, I would have taken them behind the berm and gone "old school." I actually threatened to do that to the wealthiest mentor.

During the rage of losing a contract and making a mistake, he merely looked at me patiently. His calmness infuriated me more until he laughed and said, "Thom, you never teach people how to make money until you teach them how to learn or give them a foundation to learn. I assumed you knew that. Worse thing you can ever do is give people money or access to money if they don't learn to earn it or have a foundation in place to use it once earned. I thought you were smarter than that. If the Navy just handed some kid a SEAL trident without the training and earned foundation, they would destroy the SEAL teams in about a month."

As he spoke the truth, I knew he was right, and truth stings. Earn it, build a foundation, and don't hack the system has always been my way, yet I had abandoned the process wholesale. I, like so many others, chased the excitement of money and disregarded the proven basics.

The stunning truth I realized while redesigning the process and method to train the five pyramids in the proper sequence pointed to the amount of time the training would take for clients if done with priority. Each time we modeled the training and virtually executed it down to the hour and day and week and month, it took nine months.

My internal battle when realizing the process would take nine months to train one client centered on one question: "Who would commit to nine months of training?" As I viewed the news media, the millennial generation, and the advertising spectrum, I saw no appetite for long-term anything. People want a five-minute workout, Uber for food deliveries, and to hack this, cheat that as a norm and standard. Long and drawn out processes seemed completely gone from society.

Sadly, I tried to cheat my own curriculum and take aspects out and make parts more immediate and less iteratively based. Each hack we applied destroyed the measurable outcome of the longer original training. We took out all the hard homework and just made it class-room based and didactic. I gave the shortened, hacked training to one of my mentors, and he stopped me after an hour. He simply stood up and walked out. As he departed, he said, "Now you are wasting my time, because the outcome is lost." Long story short! Later I sat with him and got the best advice I had received since being in the SEAL teams.

"Success takes time. Doing things right is always a pain. If someone wants a hack to success, they are not your clients. If the training takes nine months, will they succeed? If your answer is yes, then stick to the plan. I only pay for what will produce a result! Now find out for yourself what sequence works and what the outcome will be if you do it right!"

First Blunder

Pursuing wealth first is the first blunder with regard to success in all five pyramids. And I fell directly into the same trap others before me had also fallen. The question I had to ask and also resolve was why does pursuing wealth first cause loss of wealth? I had to define wealth and then determine what caused the sole pursuit of wealth to destroy wealth over time.

I met with and interviewed 25 businesses and owners from organizations that run on three shifts, to ones that are five days a week from nine to five and ones that are more entrepreneurial. I learned there are two ways to look at any organization.

The Organization:

1. Leadership

2. Targeting markets

3. Recruiting practices

4. Training fundamentals

5. Retaining people and profit

The Leader:

1. Physical capability

2. Capacity to learn

3. Compensation for value

4. Relationships at home

5. Spiritual use

As you can imagine, most organizations require a level of comfort with a consultant prior to disclosing EBITDA and even discussing profit and loss. I realized immediately trust was required before "the books" would be opened. I also knew that profit and loss is the latent effect of the other line items and would not show how profit or loss actually occurred.

My real interest resided in the employees and their leaders. My experience in the SEAL teams showed me that the people cause the results due to effective leadership, not the market nor the product nor the service. The enemy analysis in the business sector is very effective in that the enemy is often hidden and doesn't present a clear target. In the business world the market is never clear; in fact, it requires great leaders leading in order to carve clarity out of a nebulous space. Great leaders create something from nothing.

Leadership

The six distinctions of leadership, to be frank, are very rare to find in the world.

1. Clear purpose and vision for the team or company

2. Mission statement had to be precise and measurable

3. Team or company organized around actions and compensation for those actions

4. Wicked smart about their field

5. Composure during loss

6. Energetic at all hours of the day

Vision and mission are the sole responsibility of the leader. Leaders have to speak it, live it, and reinforce it every single day, 7 days a week, 365 days a year. Leaders who do not have these two points of responsibility cause more damage than do an earthquake and forest fire combined.

The third line item is accountability. The leader doesn't do the work. The *team* does the work. In order to be an effective leader, the team's actions, or individual employee actions, has to be spelled out in as detailed degree as possible. And a compensation plan also has to be spelled out to the same level of detail. The leader holds the team accountable for actions they have agreed to do, and the leader compensates the employee only for what they actually do.

Line items four through six are a character analysis of the leader, who the leader "is" that is always on display. Number five, composure during loss, I have found to be the most critical character flaw in leadership. This line item makes or breaks a leader, a team, a company, or even a country. It is rarely taught, because everyone wants to win, and no one considers teaching someone how to lose. And line item five is the most covered up, hidden, "no one talk about it" bit of information needed to be discovered in a company.

Immediately, I recognized that, unlike the SEAL teams, not everyone has a clear, articulate identification with both the vision and mission of the organization. My preconceived notion was that everyone would be able to recite the vision and mission statements that the boss had or possibly that there be a written statement on display throughout the company space as a reminder.

What I discovered was that was not the case at all. Sixteen of the 25 had no vision and mission statement on display other than in an email or on a brochure. And, oddly enough, of the 16, the sample of employees from CEO to receptionist, only three could articulate the vision and mission. Maybe it didn't matter because the employees still went to work every day and made money and had a building to work in?

However, of the nine companies who could clearly articulate the vision and mission, all nine—from the CEO to the receptionist—could spell it out word for word. There were posters up across the organization, and who they were and what they did was very clear. Maybe it had an effect?

The compensation for specific actions was rather disturbing. To this very moment of writing down what I learned, I remain disturbed at the compensation plans I witnessed during the process of interviews. Five companies had clear documentation of roles and responsibilities and compensation plans that did not deviate. The remaining companies were sketchy: sketchy in every sense of gray . . . nebulous, deceptive, and cover-ups. Without clarity, money was paid for actions not completed out of the leader's emotional baggage and fear of losing the employee. Often the employee excused themselves with grand tales and reasons worthy of "Emerson." In short, actions were never completed yet pay came anyway.

Target Markets

There are three types of ways to engage both the enemy in the military sector and markets in the business sector. In either sector you have to have a level of experience gained from utter failure: The fact is that you cannot play in every market effectively. Just because there is an enemy or markets doesn't mean you go after it. That same experience will also inform you of the reality regarding "never try to please everyone." Winners engage one market really well; losers play in all markets and always struggle. In the military the same is true, patrolling just to draw fire causes attrition. Conversely, highly analyzed targets are very tactically and strategically efficient. The difference is target markets cost money and require intelligence while a "go after everyone" mentality requires laziness and little money.

The three markets can best be expressed in terms of **generalized markets, geographic markets,** and **specific markets.**

In the military, the markets are the same, and different units with different skill sets deal in each separately. The reason for this skill set and market-focus approach is simple. Generalized markets require just basic skills and are very dangerous, so the military throws higher volumes of basic trained soldiers at the market: low impact, high risk, and high attrition.

Geographic markets are centered on a region. The soldiers receive more training for the environmental challenges and types of engagements based on the region. Fewer soldiers receive the training. The increased skill set allows for the various dangers of the geographical market to mitigate: medium impact, risk reduced due to mitigation, and medium attrition. The specific market focus requires the highest level of training because the targets could be anywhere at anytime.

Specific markets/targets demand intense scrutiny to literally cull the exact target out of the noise of the market. Only a few soldiers are capable, yet the impact is very high (and oddly the risk is lower), and the attrition of the soldiers is really low.

Don't misunderstand what risk is. Obviously, from the point of view of life or death, war is always high risk. But mitigating risk is the key. Being selective in targets mitigates risk through analysis. Selecting the people through detailed training mitigates risk quite a bit. Having the best resources and technology cuts risk even further.

In the business sector the markets looked exactly the same. Yet, in business, a fourth market reared its ugly head. The fourth market is called "hope." I can find no other word that describes the sheer nonsense of the market. Hope in business is the process of not being prepared or trained, not knowing what to do or how to do it, but going out and trying to do something. Hope is a religious term that has a completely different contextual meaning in religion and should never be used in combat or business. Hope in business causes despair and epic failure. But there was hope anyway. Hire people and hope it works, but do nothing to prepare them.

The same five companies that had proper leadership also had the detailed specific market approach to business. Ten companies centered their markets on geographic regions. Five organizations approached their markets through the low training generalized pathway. Five used hope: no plan, no training, and a see-what-happens approach.

Recruiting Practices

I consider recruiting the number one indication of success in any endeavor in life. You are either fighting to recruit new business or fighting to bring new people into your organization or you are barricaded inside of your effort, lying to yourself and your partners that the organization will endure forever. Not only do great leaders have this in their DNA but also the whole organization needs to reflect this desire to recruit. Recruiting means growth and new ideas.

Don't be confused that the size of a company has anything to do with recruiting and the intense fight to recruit new clients and team members. Whether an organization hires new employees or brings on new clients simply isn't as vital as the underlying desire to recruit.

As with all team endeavors, the first person responsible for recruiting is the CEO, or leader. Basically, the story on recruiting should end there, with the boss always fighting to recruit new talent and clients. Tragically, that is where the story begins to take an irreconcilable turn away from recruiting toward isolation.

The second step in the effective process of recruiting is setting a very high standard for the people you are fighting to get in front of and to recruit. You need to have a distinctively clear set of parameters, such as humble, hungry, and wicked smarts. Successful recruitment tests for these three traits. Humble means how many times have they failed and how many times they got back up and tried again. Hungry means the person has an appetite for the work life, for hustle, for the long hours, or for the environment in which the business resides. "Wicked smarts" refers to this notion: "Can this person demonstrate two characteristics?"

—One, show me what you have learned so that I can gain from your experience.

—Two, more importantly, show me how to make something very complex, very simple.

The third in the triad of recruiting isn't actually the numbers; it isn't actually how many you recruit. Why? Because numbers can be distorted, irrelevant, and often reflect a disease growing in the first and second parts of recruiting. The third aspect is who is actually being compensated for actively recruiting within the corporation. Literally, who is getting paid to recruit?

Oftentimes, compensation for recruiting does not get cleared up; therefore, recruiting dies rather quickly. In organizations with less than 10 employees, the compensation plan for recruitment is rarely a contractual obligation. Small companies farm out or hire headhunters or outside agents to find people. Midsized companies, with over 10 and less than 100 employees, may also hire out the recruiting activities, but they must begin to realize the salient point of compensation. They realize someone now has to be responsible and directly compensated for actual numbers behind any and all activity regarding recruiting. Large companies must have an internal recruiting team, chaired by the CEO, with clear money assigned to achieving actual recruitment numbers.

The three factors of recruiting—CEO driven, high standards, and compensation—seem agreeable and simple to understand. During the time I spent interviewing and dealing with the 25 organizations, I found recruiting to be the most neglected aspect. Two of the 25 companies displayed the three factors. Twenty companies were reactive only . . . reactive in the sense that they only sought new clients or new hires when they lost one or the other. Those 20 companies "farmed out" recruiting or they quickly assembled a short-term team to attack the problem. Both were given a stipend. The remaining three companies had not hired a new employee or gained a new client in three years. The three were comfortable where they were. Everyone did the same work every day. The clients they did have were also comfortable.

Training Fundamentals

The old saying "everything dies in execution" belies the one hidden factor about success, not only in business but also in health, relationship, and even in hobbies: If you are not willing to train at an exercise by doing the same thing for 10,000 iterations, you will never know if you could succeed. Training the fundamentals is everything regarding success. The more you train, the better you get is not a cliché.

My first year in the SEAL teams, I shot over 200,000 rounds from various weapons. We worked out every single day, and we practiced the basics of tactics so often I wondered when I was going to learn something "high speed." After 10 years, I gave up looking for high speed and quick techniques, because I witnessed all the veterans and top guys in each skill set never did anything but basic skills.

When I finally led my platoon into combat in Afghanistan, all we did was practice and rehearse the basics in preparation for actual missions. On the missions, no matter how outnumbered and over-whelmed we were, all we did was apply the basics we had learned in training. Now, that may be a surprise to some.

The fundamental truth of success is "train the basics" relentlessly, not until you get it right but until you get the basics wrong. Then, make sure you do the basics again, because that is why things went wrong.

Great training programs have these three properties: learnable, it-erative and gradable, and intentionally tested against real life. When on-boarding someone new, you have to ensure what you are going to teach him or her is something that can be learned. Not all things can be taught and learned through a process. For example, you can teach anyone what to say; that aspect is learnable. However, you cannot teach people when or in what instance to say what they have learned. That type of learning is experience based and not basics.

When training the basics, the process must be iterative and grad-able, simply because people learn best by doing things repetitively. Experience shows no real effective hacks outperform basic iterative learning. For example, if you are hiring a new salesperson, give them a script and make them memorize it. Then make them recite it to you until they get it right and can say it without any hesitation. The pro-cess will take 100 or more iterations. Most refuse to learn and self-se-lect out. Many issues with trainability arise as the person fumbles and gets emotional regarding the recital and refuses to try again. Some will make a mistake; take your guidance and try again and again and again. Doing simple things always weeds out the uncommitted.

Once they have proven they have it, give them a test that best resembles the real world as possible. They must pass this test to move forward or be hired. On average, most new hires will fail a graded test three to four times. Training and hiring through iterative failure are the most efficient ways to build a culture of success. The corporate world has seemed to abandon the proven process.

The final element of a training program is to ensure what you are teaching is already proven by the leaders and top people to be effective. The training has to work in the real world. Ninety percent of new hires are brought in to fill a position in which the company already knows what is needed. The company has a process and method which works, and more people following the process are needed. I acknowledge that some people are hired to bring new thoughts and new ideas to a company, yet that is another process of hiring.

For some unknown reason, I have yet to pin down why constant training in the fundamentals is not yet a staple for organizations. All 25 organizations I worked with did have professional and very knowledgeable employees in each position. There was no lack of successful people who did their jobs really well. Not one organization had a process to teach or pass on the experience to new hires in an efficient manner or with purpose.

I did see 25 uniquely different on-boarding and initial training programs. The wide range of programs was expected, yet the clearly visible success rates and viable offerings were shocking. Disturbing, in that having gone through the training myself, I graduated into a confused environment with no oversight or guidance. Even worse, if I had been paid once I was through, I would be a liability to the team and company. I would not be a valuable asset at all.

In the end there were only two trainings that taught me exactly what I needed to know to help the organization, and I could have begun working upon completion. Each of these successful training programs required four weeks of intense iterative learning and execution. Each day demanded me to prove I had learned a skill and could demonstrate that specific skill. At the conclusion of each day, there were things to memorize and assignments due. Skills and techniques were demonstrated to me, and I had to prove to the trainer I could do each skill. In effect, the successful training programs were difficult, and I had to prove myself. The most profound point of these two on-boarding programs was that they were the only ones where I, or the new hire, had to pay money to participate.

A quick breakdown of the other programs is best served by separating them into four categories, ranked from least beneficial to immediately impactful:

1. Initial familiarization and on-the-job training. Free to the new hire!

2. Classroom based education, then a period of time to meet a threshold. Free to the new hire!

3. Off-site training provided by outside consultants to teach universal skills, then a period of time to meet a threshold. Free to the new hire, plus a stipend to attend.

4. On-site company run specific training, followed by a short period of time "under instruction", then a guided process to prove to the leaders you can do the job you are hired to do. New hire must pay for the training.

I pause here for just a moment, because training is not just a check-off-the-box item. Training is really the key to success of a company, team, or even an individual striving to excel. Detailed and difficult training is required to not do damage to the organization and new hire. Extensive training on the basics of proven methods with oversight and support is the only way. The second notion of training people is to pass on all the relevant skills that the ones before have learned, or the same mistakes will be made again and again. The third part of training is to weed out the ones who cannot perform those skills you are hiring them to perform. Those three salient points are the reasons to train people.

After going through all the different training programs and then trying to make a difference in the company as if I were a new hire, my realization was made simple. The first two methods to train new hires is equivalent to giving me a pistol and one bullet and sending me into the Amazon to see if I come out the other side. These two methods pose so many issues, I don't want to waste your time explaining them. In the end, however, I guarantee three situations arise. The first is mass attrition of the hires. Attrition is expensive. The second simply is if people make it through the Amazon (or don't make it through training), there remains no way to adjust or change training. The third and final disaster is when someone does make it through the swamp. Success here is the biggest issue for a company and the new hire. If a new hire makes it through, they are bitter, resentful, and never loyal. You left them to die and they survived, but not because of you. These people will leave as soon as they get another company to actually care about them.

Option three is when a company knows it doesn't have the time or experience to train new hires to learn generalized or specific skills, so the leaders decide to have outside agents train the organization. At first glance this makes sense and can leverage immediate returns. Oftentimes, young companies will benefit due to not having the experience or staff. Even mature companies can use this method to teach new skills that are required in the ever-changing market. But consultants are a "double-edged sword" for a company. The first cut is positive and of benefit. The second cut, rather the edge facing the company, is once the skill being taught is deemed important, the company has to have its own in-house staff trained to continue the training. If you don't have in-house trainers take the second tranche, then the older untrained leaders or older staff will destroy the ones being trained. And consultants are very expensive unless they train the in-house staff to be trainers. The solution is quite simple. Bring in a consult to quickly train your people to a new standard or new set of skills, then have the consultant train in-house staff. Great consultants are always in the process of working themselves out of a contract by passing on their knowledge.

Option four is imperative! Option four works every time. Option four will accomplish in less time and with less expense the outcome desired. Option four requires complete ownership of what is being trained. Option four demands the ones being trained learn basics and demonstrate their ability to use the basics before the company risks pushing the new hire in front of clients. The difficulty with option four is getting to an agreement on the basics. The major hurdle in option four is being confident enough in their skills to be able to sell a new hire on spending money to learn.

In summary, 20 companies engaged in the first two training methods. The normal attrition rate in six months was 70 percent of the new hires. Two companies used option three to great effect because they didn't have the staff and did have the money to pay for outside consultants. Their success rate was the reverse 80 percent retention in six months, and the new hires actually could impact the company on day one after training. Three companies used method four. They took each new hire through rather strict training protocols. Each trainee failed many times before the staff cleared them to be ready. Each new hire reported a deeper sense of culture and connectivity to the company as a whole. Each trainee actually graduated from the training. The 92 percent graduation rate and 100 percent retention for one is unheard of. And option four cost the company nothing. The reverse was actually the case: the training program actually made the company money both from the direct payment of the new hire, and during training the new hire made money.

Retaining People and Profit

Bottom-line up front . . . culture. A company culture is ultimately measured in the retention of great people and the retention of profit. Culture isn't how an employee "feels" about the company as the company loses profit or makes it. Culture isn't how homogenous or diverse the employees are.

Culture is leadership's capacity to articulate a clear vision, maintain a measurable mission, and compensate people for actions that contribute to the company's mission. Culture is working on a team with a specific target in sight and coordinating all activity around that target. Culture is the distinction of recruiting and selecting the right people for the right job on the best team. Culture is solidified by training and passing on what works and ensuring everyone in the organization proves capability and improves themselves every day. How someone feels inside may have nothing to do with culture of success in your organization. Conflict, stress, long hours, losses, and failures are the weekly dynamics of success. And the failures feel horrible when passing through them. Good leadership, effective recruiting, and difficult training cause stress and conflict, yet the culture of teamwork overcomes the feelings every single time. Culture is measured by the retention of people and profit.

Culture of Outcomes

After the six-month exercise in defining wealth, a clear delineation between successful pursuit of wealth and the tragic bloodletting of failure stood out. The creating and reinforcing of a company culture from the CEO to the janitor made a huge difference. I had to ask myself what I had missed in my first attempt to train clients that I now saw as an advantage. What actions did the top two companies have that the others simply did not have?

The only way to find that out was to ask the leaders and then ask the team. If the two answers were the same, would my theory convert to reality? I learned this process of simplicity in the SEAL teams. I have to admit I hated every one of my platoon chiefs when they told me to get the ground truth, to just look for facts and never feelings. Their way of saying it is straightforward: "Go find out. If you cannot taste it, then don't bring it back. If you didn't put your eyes on it, it didn't happen. And, if you cannot pick it up and show it to me, then it isn't real."

My first efforts were to interview the bosses of the companies and ask, then determine the tangibility of their answers. Once complete, the next efforts were to do the same with the employees.

Good Companies

Bosses' questions and answers

1. What is your main responsibility in the company? Recruit and retain great people to produce measurable results.

2. What makes your organization successful? Selecting markets and products and ensuring the people are capable of doing their jobs.

3. What do you do differently than other companies? We develop the whole employee. We care about their families and ensure they are healthy and give them opportunities to grow. This makes all the difference. You can train anyone to do a task, but you have to give your people opportunities to have a great life too.

Employee questions and answers

1. What is your main responsibility in the company? To do my job and support my team.

2. What makes this company successful? We know what we are doing and don't waste our time.

3. What does this company do differently than others? We work as a team and my family and outside life matters to my boss.

Bad Companies

Bosses' questions and answers

1. What is your main responsibility in the company? To make a profit and position the company to sell or maintain the business.

2. What makes your organization successful? Great products and adjusting to market demands.

3. What do you do differently than other companies? Keep costs low and have a good benefits package.

Employee

Employee questions and answers

1. What is your main responsibility in the company? To do my job.
2. What makes this company successful? The company sells service and products lower than the market.
3. What does this company do differently than others? Is close to home and can work overtime if needed.

The Key to Culture

The main issue regarding why just improving the processes and day-to-day functions of a company ultimately causes loss is the gray area of culture. Improving processes inside of an organization without addressing the needs and issues of the life of the employee outside of the business causes stagnation. Every employee from boss to janitor notices the stagnation or, rather, the impression that working harder doesn't always increase profit but always decreases family and lifetimes. Often the notion to "double down" at work seems to be the only solution. Once this course of action and follow-on activity commences, the outcome is certain. Each employee's health and relationships at home suffer. Sales may improve in the short term, yet the analogy of pouring three gallons of water into a two-gallon bucket never seems to add up to three gallons retained in the bucket. There is always the perception of a drain or hole that leaks out water, or all the effort never makes a difference.

The wise leaders who realize that not only does taking care of the employee at work do well, but also simultaneously training and leading in efforts to ensure physical health and employee key relationships at home are being addressed win the long game. The leaders win through creating, demonstrating, and ensuring the overall culture is really what they lead. That culture is employee health, employee key relationships, and ultimately, employee work satisfaction.

The ultimate truth in the chaos of leadership is that everything counts. The notion of leading everything seems even more chaotic, but in reality, is less so. I had to ask myself the simple question of "Was the all-inclusive life of a Navy SEAL trainable, learnable, and even impactful in a corporate environment?" Would showing leaders how to be responsible to their health, their learning, their business, their key relationships, and their spiritual growth ensure sustainable growth in everything? Yet my peeling back the layers that prevented an "everything" approach would expose weaknesses.

Efficient Time Management

During the process to unravel the number of meetings both the company may have a day or each week and how many the senior staff had, I realized another key element of generating wealth. Meetings either destroy time, or they accelerate results. There seemed to be no in betweens. Too many meetings take too much time and the results of the organization suffer. Worse still was the fact that 3 out of 25 companies never have a meeting on a daily basis.

The companies who had no meetings on a daily basis were also the companies whose employees could not articulate the vision or mission statements. Yet again, the impact may not matter to overall success. I had to consider that when a company is the only one in town offering a service or product, then poor leadership and lack of training of employees pales in comparison to the reality of the job being the only one in town.

After sitting through hundreds of meetings over the weeks with multiple companies, a pattern of effect did emerge. Every single employee requires contact and clarity on a daily basis, whether it be by phone call, text or email, or an actual meeting. The earlier the meeting or contact, the more productive the employee and the organization, measured by results and outcomes that day. The inverse also became clear: the more the meetings, the less the results, and the later in the day, the less results.

That simple truth seemed clear to me. Yet time and meeting management was a complete paradox to the company. I literally sat in multiple meetings a day in the same organization. The paradox is that 18 of the 25 companies spent 35 percent of their days in meetings.

Another key point was witnessing the various meeting times of the boss. Each meeting where the boss attended lasted more than 60 minutes; some often lasted 90 minutes. Many meetings were spent regurgitating data and required no decisions from the boss. If I were to negatively impact a leader, I would ensure the leader was in meetings which had no decision points and were just social gatherings and lasted more than 20 minutes. Meetings break the boss's life by taking too much of his or her time! I also realized I could destroy a company and a leader by having the meeting center around the leader organizing the company instead of the direct reports briefing the leader on organized action items that required his or her decision. Just focusing on business activities and deemphasizing health and family. Doubling down on work causes problems that cannot be solved at work. Leaders need to conduct meetings to ensure the mission is clear, empower direct reports to execute, and to lead the all-inclusive space of the holistic life of the employee.

Solving Sequence When a Leader's Time is out of Control

Great mentors always make things harder, it seems. Great teachers always make the person dealing with a problem to "own it" without covering up the dirt. I had to expose the chaos of out-of-control time management, too many direct reports, and an employee culture of despair. The process became solidified in that moment when I became clear that the process had to be in sequence, had to be earned by actions done through repetition, and had to take at least nine months.

The question I had to ask was "How do I get leaders to commit to nine months when I had not ever done the new sequence with a leader?" I had no evidence to support my assumptions. The only way to prove the process out was to do it myself. I had to own it and work through each of the details and achieve the particular results I had suggested in order to prove results.

Long ago the SEAL teams realized there were three measurable—and two intangible but "can't succeed without them"—traits they wanted in a warrior in combat. In the organizations that prospered during my own research, these five unique areas break out of the complexity of chaos. The three measurable traits were the physical ability of the warrior; the ability of the warrior to adapt and learn; and the ability of the warrior to achieve results or derive personal value. The two intangible aspects, why the warrior was there in the first place, were the warrior's relationship with immediate family and the state of his or her spiritual life.

Each of the five is equally important, meaning never neglect or eliminate one for another ever. Every single day you had to be responsible for engaging in activity that supports each of the five, and you had to account for those activities being done with your family and your team. I call them the five pyramids of growth.

In successful business cultures the five pyramids of growth determine culture and success. The leader had to actually take the time and do the activities in his or her life regardless of the ups and downs or demands of the day. Then, the organization had to be structured around these five pyramids for each employee. The leader had to lead by example and empower others to do the same. I had to prove out a sequential process and detailed method to create a culture within a company.

The solution I chose was to train the leader first, because the complexities involved in transforming an organization without the leader fully realizing the measurable benefits of mastering the five pyramids of human performance in their personal life would be met with resistance and more complexity. I had to simultaneously lead the training and produce the results of the training in my life as the leader applied the processes and methods in their life.

Much to the dismay of my mentors during that earlier time, I chose the risky path of mentoring the people who wanted the training while simultaneously demonstrating how I too was using the process and methods in my life. My contractual obligation spelled out that if I didn't achieve the results in my life and if the leader didn't achieve his or her results, then no money would change hands. My mentors laughed and suggested to never tie my personal results nor a client's outcome to money. They further suggested, "You should try to control someone's actions and tie those unpredictable actions to the money they will pay you."

The following 11 months, I trained seven leaders to achieve 2X results in each pyramid as I, too, demonstrated the same 2X results in my life. Risk is not a four-letter word. Risk should be spelled reward.

The Method: The five pyramids of human performance in the proper sequence of learning and applying are:

1. *Spiritual*

2. *Physical*

3. *Relationship*

4. *Wealth*

5. *Intellectual*

CHAPTER SIX

True Value: Paying Yourself for Simple Actions

The Process: Determine the value of your three simple actions. Either you value excuses or action, you cannot value both! Put a price on every action you take.

"Every action you take, every thought you think has measurable value. The true value of your life can be determined simply by putting a price on three simple things in five areas of your life and paying yourself." Thom Shea, 2016

Every action you take or excuse yourself from taking has a value. If you execute the action, it increases the likelihood of success. If you don't execute, the value decreases equally as much. In this chapter, I'll show you how to place a financial value on everything you do within the five pyramids. While you may be tempted with excuses that you don't have the time to do three simple things within each of the pyramids daily, the real battle isn't about time. When you compensate yourself (or penalize yourself) for actions you agreed to do and completed or actions you agreed to do and found excuses not to, you begin to see the value of each of the pyramids. You cannot prioritize one pyramid over another. If I was able to stick to the system while on deployment in Afghanistan, then you can certainly do it now.

The innumerable mistakes I have made and will make profoundly impact my success and the successes of my family, my team, and those whom I mentor. As you read through each section and use the process in the formula and engage in the methods described, know this simple truth: embrace your failures! Success does not come from winning. Success comes from missteps, breakdowns, and failures. Success means finding three simple things to engage in while dealing with the overwhelming complexity of chaos.

The actions you take with intention, either by omission or commission, set you up to succeed or knock you down and you quit. Failure leads to success. Quitting is not failure. Quitting is the worst disease known to mankind. Quitting destroys health, breaks up marriages, makes you feel dumb, loses money, and makes your connection to God or a divine spirit meaningless. Just stop quitting. Stop it!

The key to embracing failures in each area of your life will best be understood by putting a financial price point to every action you take in life. When the thought of putting a price on action comes to your mind, I guarantee the effort will seem like eating an elephant. Your brain will see price as too complex, too difficult, and you will take months lining out every action. Or you simply won't embrace the effort to identify and put a price on any action. Complexity is not your friend. The neuroscience and putting a price to action notion is the key to real success.

Three simple things must be implemented to change actions or execute a plan or sustain effort over time: the actions need to be taken, the reward needs to be given or pulled back, and the neurotransmitter dopamine in your brain needs to occur.

One of the wealthiest men I know showed me the technique to value actions by putting a price on each of them. He died in 2009 at age 98 with his entire family around him. Every person in his family was successful, healthy, and truly valued what they did and what they said to each other. He had not given any of them his fortune prior to his death. Each had earned their own way by using the processes and price of actions methods. In his last will and testament, he laid out ways each would earn their portions of his fortune. He valued action and put a price on it.

Determining Value

The detailed value formula passed to me is eight pages long. Every single action and thought my wealthy friend put to paper reflected a price that would be paid, and the same price would be retracted if the task or goal was not committed. For the two years he was my mentor, I witnessed him putting money in a huge barrel or taking money out of the barrel. My initial thoughts of having a barrel of money denied me the brilliance of what he had created for himself and his family. The brilliance was he and his family got to see on a daily basis what he valued by putting money into the barrel or what he did not value by taking money out.

Breaking down the complex way in which he engaged the value formula to the three simple things literally took me five months to accomplish. Looking back at my attempts to make it simple makes my effort seem futile, because in the end I presented my findings to him and he laughed and said, "You should have asked me, I would have broken it down to three things for you."

The three simple things, or thoughts or actions, are the key to the formula. Can you pay yourself to do three simple things? Do you value what you do enough to pay yourself? And is the price you pay worthy of doing it?

The real price of each action item is relative to the actual gross income the person makes, and to progress to actually paying that amount, the process and method to carve out value takes a level of commitment I only realized in 2009 after his death. A short time after his passing, I used the true value formula as well as the human performance formula and three simple things and mentorship to thrive in the chaos of combat in Afghanistan. I had to use every resource and skill I had learned in the SEAL teams and every proven process I had picked up from mentors over the years. Combat is the true test to determine if theories have any practical impact. Many theories have no practical impact; only a handful make the grade.

As I open up my field notebook from those days in 2009 to share how I designed and structured the formulas, please forgive the reflections of circumstances and events that shaped my decisions. Wartime and living in war alters your DNA in ways people who have not been there cannot imagine. For me war was like the old siren song for sailors that pulled them into dangerous waters, yet the sailors could not refuse the urge. War was that way for me: I hated and loved it yet went toward the song every day during the six-month deployment.

If I may, let me describe the chaotic world of war and of being a SEAL in combat. When you arrive into the combat zone, every single thing is a threat and not under your control for a short period of time. Rocket attacks are frequent. Funerals of dead Marines or soldiers seemed to occur every night. Food and water are a problem. Sleeping is not considered until chaos can be controlled. Your relationships back home seem to be gone forever. And worse, no matter how deeply committed you are to God or whatever religion you profess, it all seems to have abandoned you. The picture seems bleak, but it is much worse than I can express, because death lurks everwhere all the time.

Carving out three simple things takes skill, commitment, and discipline in the best of times. Without those elements, the task to find three is futile due to the constant adjustment to the environment and the constant influx of 96 more important, life-threatening things. In war, where you seem to be threatened on all fronts and out of control in all five pyramids, the only action you can take is to drop anchor, or just carve out the time and actions you know you must do. You have to make your time and actions nonnegotiable.

The three simple things and payments for value per pyramid I forced myself to carve out were as follows:

Physical (working out and going on missions is the same)

—Work out in camp or be in combat for 60 minutes a day,

—Stretch and rehab 20 minutes a day.

—Drink 10 glasses of water every day.

—Pay myself $5 for each action completed a day or take out $5 for not doing it.

Wealth (may not make sense, but combat operations were how we got paid, so in combat wealth is conducting combat missions)

—One hour a day finding the enemy

—One hour a day taking care of the team

—One hour a day building a systematic way to impact the enemy in the long term

—Pay myself $5 a day per action or withdraw $5 for believing my excuses

Intellectual

—Ten minutes learning a new tactic, technique or procedure

—Ten minutes improving on existing skills

—Ten minutes pushing a limit to see if I missed an undiscovered way to engage

—Pay myself $5 a day for learning or withdrawing $5 for thinking I was too smart to learn

Relationship (with spouse because without fail, I knew the men on the team would get time and action every day)

—Ten minutes listening to or reading what Stacy was up to that day

—Ten minutes speaking to or writing down and sending to Stacy what I was doing that day

—Ten minutes of touching or virtual intimacy with Stacy

—Pay myself $5 a day for the actions or take out $5 for causing a divorce

Spiritual

—Ten minutes a day moving every joint and muscle intentionally, then turning on and ensuring all five of my senses were ready for war, then reading my formulas

—Pay myself $5 to engage and withdraw $5 to pay the angel of death (as I call him)

Paying for Action

Therein lies the structure of value I place on my actions and, by magnitude, my life in 2009. Sadly, the price was derived from the combat pay I was entitled to in Afghanistan. The price is different now, yet the act of actually putting money in a jar or taking it out may actually be the same visceral experience. Putting the money in feels great, yet I learned during that experience to put a price on actions that reward has only short-term effect on the actions. Taking money out for not doing what I said I would expose both, the value of the action and true way I felt about doing it. The long-term impact of taking money out was more influential than putting money into the barrel. My millionaire friend discovered the most brilliant way to unravel why life felt so out of control and empty . . . the emptiness felt by not taking action in areas of life we feel have no value and which directly impact the areas we do value.

In the first week, I put each $5 investment into the barrel in my room, in spite of the operational tempo and long exhausting hours. To be quite honest, I had prepared my body and mind well during the year of training to endure the chaos of war. No excuses or reasons came to me to not do what I said I would do.

During week two, my life and point of view regarding value abruptly changed and would never be the same. In week two, we conducted our first combat mission. We all had been in combat before and had fired at the enemy and been shot at many times prior to this engagement. The explosive shift occurred during the extract phase of the operation when the battle, theoretically, is won and we were on our way to the helicopters to go home. The mission proceeded exactly as planned, even down to being exhausted like on other training missions. As my men were coming back through an alley to check in with me, which they had already done four separate times during various phases of the mission, a huge improvised explosive device detonated.

Four soldiers were in the blast zone, two SEALs and two Afghan commandos. The two commandos lost both of their legs just below the hips, a gruesome injury to witness, yet not critically disturbing to me for the simple reason I had witnessed many horrific injuries both as a combat medic and as a SEAL. The shock that affected me deeply came as one of the SEALs walked past me. He said, "Never take someone else's word that an area is safe or mine free. You promised to never compromise our abilities to make others happy."

I knew exactly what he meant, because I had agreed to fully integrate my SEAL platoon with an army Special Forces "A" team and their commandos as a show of good faith. The previous decision had felt like loaning my $30,000 rifle out to a homeless man to get food. In deciding, I even felt like saying "Let us do the deed and meet you after." I had compromised what I knew worked well for something I had no experience with.

The deep shock felt was amplified when I saw the bone fragments from the legs of the commandos embedded in the face of a SEAL I had known for 10 years. This particular SEAL I had known since he was 16. His father had supported me when I was in need. Then I had supported their family by bringing the young warrior into my platoon with the express intent to keep him alive. Dishonoring my word by allowing my actions and decisions to veer from what I had promised felt horrific. And I leaned over to him and said, "I made the mistake and I will not do that ever again!"

Once back at base, after eating a good meal and spending time debriefing the men and writing reports to my bosses, I found myself back in my room looking at my list of three basic things. The physical and wealth and intellectual all were very easy to check off and put money in the barrel. The desire to engage in relationship even virtually was absent. The pain of trying to explain to my wife what I had allowed to happen was quite real. So I excused myself from any of the three simple actions from happening and went to sleep. I had convinced myself sleep would solve the pain and embarrassment of what I knew I must share with Stacy. I had excused myself from relationship without even realizing the impact.

Later that day, around lunch, my hunger pains woke me up and I immediately went to eat. All this may seem reasonable and normal under the circumstances of war. The reactivity of going to bed because I was overwhelmed and the urgency to eat seemed normal to me. At lunch with several of my platoon mates, the thought occurred that I had forgotten and dismissed three of the three simple things. I walked back to my room to take $15 out of the barrel and write down in my notebook my reasons. My excuses were tired, embarrassed, Stacy doesn't need to know, and spiritual doesn't matter.

Reaching in and taking out the money that was already there, leaving the empty space behind, I realized that because I had not done spiritual before I went to sleep and had excused myself upon waking, it revealed an excuse I now see as the most destructive dialogue to ever apply to any aspect of my life. I had excused myself because I had succumbed to the excuse called "this is stupid" or "doing this is meaningless." I sat there with nothing to show of value. My success in a few of the pyramids had been negated by excusing myself from the others.

The old millionaire must have encountered the same disturbing trend of actions and value and payment in his own life at an early age. I placed no value at all in my relationship and spirituality after the disturbing events of the day before. My reactivity to my environment literally excused me from any previous value I had placed on my wife, my family, and to God or my spiritual capacity. Devaluing things had happened so quickly, I actually laughed out loud in the small room I was in.

I sat there trying to explain to my stupid self why I had not done what I said I would do. I tried to write down my "why" hoping that seeing it written would make sense to me so I could convince Stacy of my misstep. After an hour, the last reason why made the most sense. The only reason why anyone does anything good or bad simply is "because they said they would." Even not doing something the answer is "because I said so." I had not done relationship nor spiritual because I had told myself not to. It was that simple. No external pressure, no loss of limbs, no disgusting reason explained why more than "because I said so."

I could tell myself to do it now because I said so! So I opened my computer and logged into a chat with Stacy and began to type. Stacy was surely sleeping, but I asked her how her day was going. And waited, not knowing if there would be a reply. After five minutes, I typed a brief description not of what yesterday had been like, but instead what I was going to do today and what I had learned about my "why" statement. With no response to listening and sharing, I just commented that touching her makes me feel good and that I can close my eyes and imagine her there. Engaging in relationship doesn't have to be perfect, but doing nothing at all showed Stacy no value at all. I closed my computer, picked up $15, and dropped the value of my actions into the barrel.

Throughout the next three months, no matter the operational tempo, no matter how I felt about my actions, or how tired I was, the $5 for each action got deposited. The effort to deposit instead of making a withdrawal was painful. Painful in the sense that the battle inside of me wasn't with doing the actions but was in excusing myself and pushing off all the reasons not to do them. The three simple things were easy to actually do. The thousand reasons not to do them crippled me.

The war going on inside seemed so real and so convincing. Some-times the physical things were very painful to actually do. Many a day, I would have pain medication and therapy as a method to stave off pain from dictating activity. Often, taking the time to learn dropped in priority to just doing things the way they were always done. I had to set an alarm on my watch to remind me to engage in learning so I would not forget. I never heard the excuse of lack of support, simply because the entire platoon was immersed and committed to finding, fixing, and finishing the enemy. I am proud of my wife for supporting me in combat. Had she not supported my being a SEAL in combat, the entire effort to go to war would have been immensely difficult. The feedback and value I did receive from engaging the three simple things of relationship with Stacy and often the kids may have provided the real foundation to keep in the fight. Had she, even once, inferred what I was doing was stupid, I would have stopped doing it a second later. The morning and evening spiritual activity I made nonnegotia-ble! Whether I was on a mission or back in camp, I did not allow any internal or external battle to keep me from intentionally moving every part of my body, ensuring all my senses were engaged, and reading my five formulas.

The barrel of money began to fill up with value. Then we conducted a mission where death seemed to truly want to take us all. We were overrun, we ran out of bullets. During the 45-minute firefight, I was hit in the chest plate twice, had two bullet holes in my pants, and got knocked out by a rocket-propelled grenade. We had literally fought for our lives. The experience left me broken outside and inside. And that fact was hard to admit while I was in charge and still active duty. I could not even speak of it to my wife for a week.

Once back at camp, safely in my room, I watched as what seemed like someone else's hand withdrew $75 a day. I couldn't seem to stop the withdrawal, which meant I could not get back in the game at all. Nothing mattered any more. I didn't care to be in combat. I didn't want to be married. My reasons and excuses were so subtle and seductive and believable. I never thought of suicide, but I do know why people in that same state of mind would convince themselves to end it all. The reasons really make sense.

That morning, eight days after we returned from Hell, I decided to get my rifle and take it to the range and shoot. I knew I had to "get back on the horse," and I also knew shooting would remind me of my fun childhood years of hunting deer. But the gun felt odd in my hands and only brought back thoughts of near death. My body still hurt, and getting into a shooting position was remarkably uncomfortable. No one wanted to go with me, and the lack of support was difficult to handle. After the first round impacted the target and missed where I was aiming, I became aware of how out of touch I was. I forced myself back into the form and technique of sniping that I had learned and practiced for 18 years. As the final round impacted and my grouping was exactly what I wanted, everything seemed to come back into focus. The drive back to the camp felt like I was alive again and the excitement to get fully engaged in all aspects of my life flooded my mind and body. The excuses vanished, and all that remained was the three simple things.

The deployment did end. All my men had not only survived but also thrived in the chaos of combat. We had cut through the complexity of war outside of us and had won the battle of internal excuses. My barrel of money I had invested into the things I valued was full.

Baseline Value

The impact of paying yourself for three simple things changes you in two remarkable ways. You need not go to combat to see the impact. You only need to write down your three simple things and attempt to do them for 21 days straight. You will discover the first impact simply by identifying three simple things out of the complexity of the millions of seemingly important things you face. That effort will get you in action and create momentum no matter how stuck you are, how old you are, or in whatever state of success you find yourself.

The second and most difficult impact will be the killing off of your excuses that you apply to everything you do in your life. You will have to stop reasoning yourself out of your own success. Excuses are so seductive and believable, but you will have to do battle and win this war to achieve simplicity. Self-discipline literally means to pay no attention to excuses and reasons and honor your word no matter what comes up. A nonnegotiable life of three simple things in all five pyramids a day makes life quite extraordinary.

I also found out there are several of the three simple things that are difficult to not excuse myself from doing. And all of the clients I have mentored through the training express the same issues and excuses. As you learn the process of the formula and the methods of applying the training, take note of what we have learned.

The first area of concern, for men and women alike, is putting financial value on three simple things in relationship. Paying yourself for taking 30 minutes out of your day to listen, speak, and be intimate takes one month to complete. Clients report these reasons to excuse themselves for engaging, and therefore putting any value into their relationships:

—I already know what he or she will say.

—I don't have the time.

—This is stupid and of no value.

—They don't support me, or I don't support them.

—I don't know what to say.

—I am too old for childish intimacy.

—I forgot.

All the reasons make sense to the person having them. I have even witnessed clients getting friends to support their excuses by telling them "that is a waste of time" or "who needs the pressure of a spouse knowing your business." My warning as you engage in simplicity is to do the math. No matter how well you engage wealth, you take out the same value by doing nothing in relationship. Relationship takes 30 minutes and wealth takes three hours to achieve a baseline. Just look at the numbers. More to the point is to consider how stupid you are for using the excuse "I don't have the time" and working all day then taking the value of your work out of the barrel by devaluing relationship and not engaging even one of the three simple things.

The true value of your life isn't just making money through work alone. If that is all you do, you will see a huge deficit in the barrel. The baseline equation to learn is each action represents the same price. Obviously, most people only experience value by getting paid for the work they do. Imagine if you paid yourself for each pyramid and each of the three simple things. You will experience the true value and financial upside of your life. If you don't engage each pyramid or put a price to anything other than work, you will feel like you have to work longer and harder, and the more you work, the more you feel you have to double down and work more.

Imagine what you will be capable of doing when the true value of all of your five pyramids of performance is realized once you put a price on everything you do?

The first experiment with the true value formula that has made the biggest difference in the lives of my clients comes from the 21-day challenge to learn to compensate yourself for the actions you provide or, in each case, for the actions you previously agreed to do. The price of the initial actions during the challenge need not represent anything to you. To make that challenge easy, simply use the $5 per action price point. Even if it is $1, the struggle with excuses will disturb you.

The price is relative to what you actually bring in due to the job you have. For example, if your gross income is $100,000 per year, that is how much you are compensated for the value you provide. For me, that is the true definition of wealth.

The full true value formula we have set up over the years of working with high achievers is quite different. Each of the five pyramids has a different number of actions to accomplish other than the three simple things. The formula contains 30 separate actions.

True Value Formula

Spiritual (turn on each five senses, read each formula for the five pyramids, and execute on three simple things) = 13X

Relationship (focus, let go, fail, mentor, three simple things, speak your goal, and know their goal) = 7X

Physical (focus, let go, fail, three simple things) = 4X

Wealth (focus, let go, fail, three simple things, and compensation) = 5X

Intellectual (Learn one new thing and apply it to one pyramid) = 1X

Each x-factor of the 30 actions counts the same. The most cumbersome backpack to carry in your life regarding true value and real wealth is the struggle with the various actions of your life where you have yet to put a price on the action. Over the past six years of working with my mentors as well as several applied mathematicians, we settled on the true value formula to show the 30 points of performance.

I, too, was stunned when the mathematicians who completed the yearlong training presented me with the formula. The explanation made perfect sense, even to the point of recognizing where efficiency and effectiveness need be applied and rarely are. As you read and digest the formula, note the new x-factors I have not discussed. The elements of focus, let go, and fail represent the tools of performance. The tools of performance take six months to teach and possibly more time to learn. Yet, the formula simply recognizes they represent actions that have measurable value and clearly impact the outcome.

When clients begin the training, they begin from a condition I refer to as an "unbalanced life." Unbalanced in the sense that both times spent and actions done in each pyramid demonstrate a lack of understanding of where true value comes from. Like you, most people spend a majority of the day chasing wealth and neglect the other four pyramids. If you are one of those types of people, please recognize that when you neglect spiritual and relationship, you create a value deficit that wealth and intellectual and physical can never overcome. Since most people find themselves in this unbalanced condition, the feeling is to double down on the time spent learning, working, and engaging in health. The deficit remains, nonetheless.

The battle isn't time. Don't go down the path to figure out how to get more time. You cannot get more time. The battle isn't choosing between one of the other pyramids. The futile pursuit of prioritizing one over the other will leave you bitter and resigned, yet most people attempt to pick and choose one over the other. The battle needs to be fought in establishing a nonnegotiable baseline of carving out time, engaging the tools, and ending with three simple things. The battle is truly between honoring your word or succumbing to your excuses. The excuses push you to only engage one or two pyramids a day. You will never know the true value of your life if you succumb to your excuses.

The Method: The true value of your life comes from paying for the actions you take every day. The X-factor formula. "X" = Gross yearly income / 365 / 30.

1. Spiritual upside is 13X

2. Physical upside is 4X

3. Wealth upside is 5X

4. Intellectual upside is 1X

5. Relationship upside is 7X

CHAPTER SEVEN

A Nonnegotiable Life

The Process: Determine how much time and
what activities during the day need to be nonnegotiable.

Time and Energy

The inescapable truth regarding success in any endeavor is the expense of time and of energy. How much time will I need to succeed? How much energy and resources will I need to succeed? Your genetics alone will never cause success to grow. Born into family or society or even having a college degree can never, by itself, bring success to you. Being handed a trophy clearly does not cause the recipient to be successful the next time at bat. Winning the lotto without a series of methods or a sustainable process surely isn't success. Actually, the aforementioned idiopathic instances cause failure. So how much time and energy are you willing to give to success?

Success takes time. Success burns energy and resources. The critical question to ask is how much of both? Scary as the question may seem, the examples of success in health, wealth, relationships, or in all five pyramids are fractured. When you look at success, as a general rule you look at number one in a category, or who has the most. That view of success is merely a snapshot of the time equation and shows nothing of the energy or resources expended to finally succeed.

As my physical mentor always reminds me, "Most people die on Everest on the descent, so don't get all excited by the five minutes of being on top. Play the entire journey out from beginning until you are home with your wife."

For instance, you may look at the CEO or a general or admiral as a success and on top. Maybe you observe and notice the number one swimmer or runner or even fighter, and since they are number one, you pin down success to them in particular. The fractured way of looking at success through the lens of "number one" will forever burden you with the herculean effort of time and energy to attain the condition of number one. Being number one is only one step, a snap-shot in time.

Through those lenses alone, success takes 30 years to become a leader, may take 15 years to be best in class athletically, and takes a lifetime to be married and a parent. Success itself then becomes a bur-den. "No one wants to spend that amount of time doing anything," you may say. The simplicity of looking at time and energy from a base-line perspective will give you access to sustaining both short-term and long-term successes. What are the baseline elements of time and ener-gy that are nonnegotiable?

We are defining success as the ability to stay engaged from begin-ning to end. Success is maintaining a nonnegotiable, six-hour base-line of using time and energy. From the point of view of looking at how much time and energy one would need to become successful, you have to abandon the long and short game. You have to throw off immediacy and even answering the question of "Is the end worth the expense?" You have to abandon your "why" statement. Nothing else matters regarding time and energy more than setting up a framework of what is nonnegotiable. To be exact, you must set aside six hours of time and energy expense that cannot and will not be dropped. You must have a nonnegotiable baseline!

Disrupting Chaos

After retiring from the Navy SEAL teams, I was brought in to consult with a leader of an organization that was "stuck," as the leader would point out. Erik leads a rather successful wealth management firm. Over the course of 28 years, he bootstrapped the business and grew from a solo practice to multiple agents with numerous staff across the nation. By all accounts well-managed, effectively led, and growing, Erik reached out to me after a keynote speech I conducted regarding "Thriving in Chaos." As I told Erik, "Success by definition is how to deal with multilayered chaos by executing simple actions." As we discussed his life, his organization, and his direction, the chaos of highly successful people became abundantly clear.

Chaos in the SEAL teams is normal, and life for each SEAL is organized and constructed around simplicity in order to deal with combat and chaos. Combat, too, conjoins multilayered chaos with bullets literally aimed directly at you. These conjoined twins of the chaos of combat incessantly pound you into focusing on immediate and urgent choices. Timelines, people, requirements, environmental impacts, live or die choices, exhaustion . . . more is always needed and less is always at hand: these are the chaotic aspects of leading men in combat. Chaos in combat cannot be avoided, it must be embraced. The only things to embrace are simple, tangible things in your life. You embrace your health, your family, and your team; you embrace learning and your job; and you embrace your human spirit. You make promises and keep them . . . even though you may die in the process.

Navy SEALs, like no other group, use chaotic environments to facilitate one key point: focus on simplicity. After 23 years of chaos and weeding out the erroneous parts from the simple parts, two realities emerged. The first reality of chaos I heard was in Erik's descriptions of what he experienced, which he overwhelmed at every level. The second, which truly intrigued him, was simplicity. Nothing was simple any longer for Erik, and most leaders across the nation have abandoned the simple for the complex. The impact of complexity hits with the force of a 2,000-pound bomb: heart attacks, divorces, entitled children, and no time for anything but a vacation from chaos to Europe even though across the street are sights and experiences equal to the European setting.

With each "deep dive" into the complexity of his day, I noted time was no longer referenced in any terms other than "not enough." And energy and resources took on the broad terms of not enough of either.

If you ever arrive at the place in life where you no longer have enough time and energy to get after your day, let me express my condolences to your partners, your family, or even your lover, because you are "stuffed." And Erik had arrived. Like most leaders, Erik has a personal aide. Like most personal aides, Erik's was on point, smart as a whip, eager, and loyal. Her tasking remarkably simple: Organize Erik's meetings, field and screen his emails and calls, and remind him where and when he needed to engage. Like all great aides, she planned out Erik's day from wake to sleep. She knew his mind and commitments better than he did . . . a truly remarkable aide in every sense of the word.

Erik's workday and workweek looked much like every top executive's. You may notice your day plays out just as Erik's:

—5:30 a.m. wake up, grab coffee from the coffee maker, which was programmed the night before

—6:00 a.m. drive to work begins

—6:10 a.m. scheduled call with colleague or top person

—6:40 a.m. arrive at work

—7:00 a.m. read emails, scan news cycle, read reports on desk, read notes from previous day

—7:45 a.m. meet with aide and review, validate, confirm, adjust, and get to it

—8:00 a.m. meeting with direct reports

—9:00 a.m. back to office for quick check-in with aide, reset schedule due to meeting, prepare for phone call at 9:15

—9:15 a.m. scheduled phone call

—10:00 a.m. meeting with either client or firm people

—10:30 a.m. check computer, check in with aide, organize thoughts

—11:00 a.m. scheduled meeting or phone call

—11:30 a.m. to 1:00 pm lunch

—1:00 p.m. scheduled meeting or phone call

—2:00 p.m. check with aide, check mail, look at news cycle or analytics of business

—3:00 p.m. meet with COO or CFO, reflect, adjust, discuss, schedule, prioritize

—4:00 p.m. phone call

—4:30 p.m. scheduled meet with client

—5:00 p.m. scheduled business dinner

—6:30 p.m. drive home, scheduled phone call during drive

—7:00 p.m. home

I will stop the grind reporting there. First, the amount of time spent is neither good nor bad. A 14-hour workday is the CEO standard. Success may require being awake, doing work, and dealing with conflict for three days straight without sleep. A woman may take 2 hours or 12 hours to deliver her baby. Your business may take one year or five years to turn a profit. Your marathon may take 2 hours or 4 hours to complete. The complete and unbridled truth of success is it takes time. A brilliant leader looks at time and how much is reactive and how much is nonnegotiable. For a moment, let me dissolve the notion regarding how much time is required to win, succeed, or turn something you are working toward completely around so that success is possible. Neither the methods and processes within nor any book should ever attempt to pin down the metric of time to succeed. Life and success don't have guarantee labels attached to the time tag. Avoid any and all guarantees in sales regarding time and hacks on time. Guarantees are for the uncommitted. The key is always what is nonnegotiable and what and how much do you have to adjust.

While interviewing many CEOs and top performers, a distinct pattern regarding time emerged. We all seem to negotiate time. More to the point, our days are constantly chasing and adjusting time and energy and priority. Now enter the rat race and the constant sprint of adaption of time and energy. The rat race is the grind of negotiating both time and energy toward achieving a specific goal. The constant sprinting to the finish line, the everyday adaptations, and the compromises needed to remain on the sprint are not sustainable. Something in your life has to give way or fall apart.

Somewhere along the way, everyone, and I mean everyone, bought into the notion that priority can be spelled priorities. The reference is subtle. Maybe it wasn't intentional? Maybe it made sense due to the complexity we all experience on a daily basis? Priority means nonnegotiable. Priorities mean negotiable.

The effect on Erik became clear, just as clear as the effect of this negotiable lifestyle currently has on you. Burnout comes from sprinting. Lying to yourself that you can double down on time and energy and somehow get more of both is completely absurd. We all have a 24-hour day. All of us have limited resources. Time and energy expense are two inconvenient truths.

Establishing a baseline of time and energy and learning a process using nonnegotiable methods literally creates sustainable performance. In order to set up the six-hour baseline, Erik had to be willing to disrupt his lifelong model of a negotiation and commit approach to a nonnegotiable portion of the time and energy he would apply to each day. Disruption to successful men and women always seems risky for the simple fact that disruption changes the status quo. Even though the status quo could be killing a business, destroying a marriage, or causing athletic performance to break an athlete, we humans resist change. Erik could not fathom a six-hour nonnegotiable baseline because it seemed like less when more was clearly needed.

Process and Method of Priority

Erik originally brought me in to his business to consult in order to make his leadership team more capable and to make more money. I am sure there are many consultation firms that are "symptom fixers" or just immediate problem-solvers. For me, the artificial upside of "moving furniture," or painting a pig, was simply exhausting. I have to admit I had been consulting as a "fixer" for a year and the money was really great, but the whole experience of knowing that the problem was going to come back because each problem was a symptom of one or two foundational issues that were the root cause was troubling.

Rebuilding and restructuring the foundation would have made a more lasting difference, but the process would take time and most leaders, like most teenagers, want immediate gratification and want the pain to go away without discussion. Worse still, Erik wanted someone else to solve the symptom and not discuss what was causing it. I even risked my offer being rejected at a time when I needed the money. Yet had I solely gone after Erik's symptoms, I would just be patching up my financial symptoms too. The never-ending loop was what neither of us was really committed to in the first place. I knew both the root cause and how to repair it. But few of my consulting friends were willing to join me to deal with it because the effort requires commitment and patience. A result-based consulting effort is risky, especially when negotiating for the majority of the fees to only be paid after the client reaches the specified goals.

The old saying (adjusted to today's way of thinking) kind of goes like this:

When you give a man a fish when he is hungry, you make him happy but kill him in the long run. Instead, teach him how to fish knowing he will hate you while fishing but will thrive for the rest of his life.

With that, Erik agreed to the process and methods I knew would cure the root issue of "priority" and effective use of time and energy. The commitment to learning the five pyramids of performance and the eventual three simple things a day would take no less than nine months and would have to accomplish nine specific goals. And I would have to mentor and coach him through all the common pitfalls that trip most leaders up.

Erik would have to learn the formula approach to a results-driven life! We would have to get Erik's life in order then work on his firm and staff. The first step is always to carve out the initial two hours of spiritual and physical time and make it nonnegotiable. The first effort always takes longer than expected, and as history often shows, though the three separate activities and time demands are simple, the biggest effort is overcoming excuses, reasons, and internal stagnation.

Erik had constructed his day and life around immediately getting out of bed, reading the current news, having a quick premade breakfast and coffee, and going straight to work. I knew from my time in the SEAL teams that disrupting a routine requires someone there to oversee the new activity. His wife and kids would not appreciate a crusty old Navy SEAL in their house. We both agreed to spend the first week in a hotel where he could isolate himself from other complex aspects of his life in order to control the simple portions of his own. The first seven days of waking up and engaging in the three simple things of spiritual time, 30 minutes, proved to be both powerful and calming to Erik. No excuses stopped him, and we had no drama and conflict. However, the 90 minutes of physical time and three simple things confounded me and disturbed Erik. All I would hear from Erik was "This is stupid and a waste of time," "I am too out of shape to be an athlete," "Stretching hurts," and "I need to get to work."

"Erik, work is important. Leading your company is also important. Your health is important as well. Your spirituality regarding being clear and having all your senses available throughout the day is important. Your wife and kids matter, too," I injected, because he clearly was on the verge of quitting. "You don't know the true power of honoring your word and never giving up. You escape this powerful truth by wasting all your time and effort making millions of dollars. I want that to sink in.

"You showed me you spend no time engaging in your health and have never had time for any level of spiritual pursuit, even prayer or mediation, in two years. You also shared that you and your wife have not had a date or any time together other than random sex. In the past month, you have only seen your two kids at night when they are doing homework. The issue isn't really time as you might think. The real issue is you live an excuse-driven life and can no longer make a promise and keep it in any other area of your life other than wealth creation. I can promise you two things if we continue but only one if you quit," I said, stopping to refocus my emotion and building temper.

"You made a promise to yourself four days ago to learn and apply the process and methods to build a life, not just a business. And you are now seeing that your foundation, which is honoring your word and never giving up, is nonexistent. What is it like for you to not be able to make a promise and keep it? What is it like to see how quickly you excuse yourself from that promise?" I stopped, knowing that question would sting.

"I just don't see the advantage of adding two hours of working out and stretching and doing the morning and evening stuff you showed me will make me more money," he said testily.

"Anger I understand very well," I said. "I think I could chair the board on the anger foundation of the world. I am not going to try to convince you of the process and method we are showing you, because you just convinced yourself of it. The foundation of success in all areas of life is predicated on honoring your word and never giving up. The foundation of failure is to excuse yourself, conveniently using any method possible, to get out of honoring your word. You can quit if you like; many people *do* quit. Or you don't have to resort to excuses and, like in the movie *The Matrix,* swallow the other pill and I will show you a lethal way to succeed in all areas of life. Which way do you want to go?" I edged closer to being asked to leave, yet knew the value if he chose the process and method path.

"What do you suggest I do differently?" he asked.

"Nothing different is needed. Just stop excusing yourself so easily from the three tasks you promised to do. If you cannot do the tasks required to achieve this goal, then you know the harder ones are impossible. Perhaps these same excuses that stop you here are the same ones stopping you in other areas. I bet when things seem stupid or don't make sense, you simply abandon them. I bet when you compare your body to someone else, you tend to back away because the experience is uncomfortable. All the while you tend not to do what you promised or do what it takes. That is a terrible life to lead. One of excuses and also one where you never get to keep a promise because of some absurd reason," I said.

"Do I have to start over?" he asked.

"Would you tolerate me giving you an unfinished product? I think you know my answer. You have to honor your word and uncover all your destructive excuses by executing three simple things per area for 21 days straight. Here is why: because I said so. If you don't, you won't learn what is really going on with you. If you don't, then nothing will change for you," I said.

"Now you must go home and begin again with all the complex distractions. I know what is in the way now. Your body is fully capable of becoming fit and available. Your wife and kids aren't distractions. Time isn't the issue. Your excuses have to be fleshed out and overcome by just doing it," I said. And as I stood there smiling, he all of a sudden understood.

"That hurt," he said "Do people threaten to fire you often?"

"Yes," I said. "You didn't bring me on to fluff your pillows, I suspect. I am not concerned with the opinion of people as they struggle to keep their word."

Twenty-one days later, Erik emerged from what I think was a battle with himself he had given up on winning. He overcame the most powerful demon, the one that throws up excuses like they were real every time he had wanted to try something new. The fight is like overcoming an addiction, and perhaps it is an addiction to excuses. At the end he lost 10 pounds. I had taught him no new skill or hack. We had even taken more time from his day than he was willing to give. By just doing three simple things and not excusing himself, the first goal was achieved.

The next two goals and number of months were designed to actually teach skills and reinforce behaviors by demonstrating the skills and showing him how to use them, then putting a price tag on executing the skills. As an observation, Erik was lethal for the next two months. He never missed paying himself the entire process. He ran a half marathon for the first time in his life. He went to every one of his kids' games. Most interesting was how lethal he was at work with the use of time. Erik was at work to give direction and make decisions and lead his leaders. He only worked a seven-hour day. At the end of that quarter, the sales revenue increased by 28 percent and they hired two new sales managers.

The goals are insignificant as stand-alone items. Taken as a whole, attaining all the goals had been impossible. As you consider how overweighted one area of your life has become, you would recognize the impact of reaching multiple goals while also increasing revenue at work. More to the point, Erik selected the relationship and health goals and, concurrently, a 25 percent increase in a quarter as important and worth the effort to attain.

As we sat down to scope out the work involved with injecting the training process and method to the direct reports, Erik hesitated. "You are saying the process is the same?" he asked.

"In the sense of laying down the same foundation and using the same methods, yes. The difference is each of their respective lives have to be goal centered. The wealth goal will be the interesting for you, as their boss, to flesh out. Often, when clients go through the first 21-day exercise and see what is truly possible once they overcome their own excuses, then they change their wealth goals. Yes, they could leave the position," I explained.

"I cannot afford to lose any of them right now," he interjected.

"What an odd statement. Either you see the benefit of the work we are doing, or perhaps you think dictating to someone what is import- ant is a better way," I said. "I don't think you can afford to have them not pursue a life that inspires them. Having your team lead a life of their own design makes them loyal. Maybe this is why you used to spend so much time at work because of conflict?

"Your measurable health changed," I said, grabbing his hand to get his attention. "You made more money due to the training." I squeezed to make the point. "What are you afraid of with your direct reports?" I asked, stopping because I did not want to hear the answer. Each cov- er-up of weakness comes up with drama and the rhetoric of disgust. I was not ready for the drama. Yet, I knew it was coming!

"You suck, you know that?" he said.

"I have heard that before, so it must be true! Right now, I am uniquely aware you are afraid because you smell afraid and your body is torqued. What about your crew having a great life makes you so twisted?" I cringed because the sob story of why he was the way he was and all that was about to burst forth. The cover-up that always prevents greatness. I sat back and prepared myself. I do hate that part of me that wants to pick up a brick and smash the doors shut so the excuses don't flow out. Alas, years of Stacy saying, "Just listen until the end," curb my brutality.

But he sat and looked at me for what seemed a long time. "If I had not just gone through your 21 days of excuses training, I would have tried to convince you why I needed to always be there. I don't think I fear abandonment, but maybe I do. I just put so much time and effort into each of them," he said, looking down. "All that would be a waste if they left, now that everything seems to be working."

"Good, I am glad you didn't puke all over me," I said. "Most people do at this point in training. No, you don't fear abandonment: that is nonsense. There are five primal fears. Everyone fears death, so that fear prevents life. Everyone is afraid that someone will discover they are dumb or not so "on the ball," so that fear prevents constant learning and excitement. Everyone fears the loss of money or resources, and that fear prevents accumulation of great wealth. It makes people play small. Everyone fears being alone, and that fear prevents love and joy. Finally, the greatest fear of all, which is where you are now. You fear that you are powerful beyond measure, and you really fear that others are too. That fear prevents them from being that person as much as it does you."

He stood up and walked around a bit, then finally sat back down. "If we train them and they decide to go somewhere else, then what am I to do?"

"Lord in heaven! Fear is a monster, isn't it. If I train them and they leave, then you have a partner at another location. If they stay, then there is a lot of work to do. If I don't train them, then nothing happens, they will probably leave because they feel stale. Do you want to play small and continue to micromanage every aspect? Fear of greatness will kill you eventually."

Setting up the Baseline of Time and Activity

The process and method training over the next several months was simple and iterative in nature. The greater effort continued to carve out and set the baseline of sequential activity to enable growth in all five pyramids for each person first, then the organization second. The excuses are always unique in an organization. The primary excuse in an organization centers around self-growth as being self-serving. Little does the organization or leadership truly realize that the growth of the individual must happen within the culture of the organization. Once culture of individual growth occurs, then the organization explodes.

Each direct report set up the 30 minutes of spiritual time and three simple things each morning and night in order to create intentionality and clarity. They did 60 minutes of the primary physical activity in the morning, a stretching regimen after work once at home, and drank the required 10 glasses of water without much internal and external conflict.

Carving out 30 minutes of the three simple things in relationship was like pulling teeth from a bear. During the relationship training, which takes no time at all relative to other pyramids, the company growth suffered. I always find this part of training to be quite extraordinary. Erik and I both watched and mentored each employee through their conflicts and excuses. The excuses are remarkable in that they each remain rooted in emotional attachment to prior bad experiences from the past or in other relationships. The listening aspect takes time because each direct report thought they knew their spouse. Emotions cause lack of newness and interest to discover the greatness in a wife or husband or lover. It was horrible to watch. This part of the process makes me sick to my stomach. Eventually, the letting go of emotional attachments freed up each direct report to listen for something new in their mate. Once this exercise is complete, limiting the time to 30 minutes is the harder effort. The moment each direct report made listening for 10 minutes every day nonnegotiable, the productivity and measurable success at work became very evident to Erik and me.

Most apparent are the outcomes and results measured in the retention of employees and revenue each employee generates when the six-hour nonnegotiable practice of doing three simple things every day is put into effect. Once Erik's direct reports broke through the chaos of their own excuses, each was "freed up" to be lethal at work. The efficiency and effectiveness were stunning to witness. As each direct report brought the process and various methods to the work environment to carve out three simple things, the meetings evolved into straightforward discussions reflecting three things: prospecting and securing new business, engaging and retaining existing clients, and projecting activities and scope of work to prove out the five-year objective.

More importantly, the empathy and communication each direct report displayed in engaging with each other displayed what I refer to as "the culture of loyalty." Having gone through the process of overcoming their own excuses and inertia, they remained fully aware that their coworkers were in their own internal battles as well. Erik called it empathy; I called it teamwork. Overall, a team of people who are striving together to attain something difficult must realize each member is both in an internal battle with excuses and an external battle with simple activity in a complex environment.

The culture of loyalty is best displayed when these two simple questions are the first ones asked by every member of the team or organization: "How are you doing? How can I help?"

Contrast those questions with the normal ones asked: "What happened?" "What is the problem?" and "Who is responsible for this?"

The greatest team building exercise for any organization remains overcoming personal challenges while openly communicating the personal breakdowns. Until these authentic conversations happen among each team member, very difficult challenges or goals simply can never happen. The 21-day challenge to battle your own excuses unpacks the greatest leadership skill and team building aspect of all: the battle with excuses and the baseline three simple things needed to execute a plan. Winning this battle with excuses has to be led, has to occur, and has to be discussed openly. Once every team member can honestly share their excuses for not doing what they said they would do, such as "I forgot," "This hurts or I am exhausted," "This is stupid," or "I don't have support," the team will never produce the results desired. Not in order to validate the lack of action but to expose the excuse.

Erik struggled with this critical aspect of building a team and leading them during chaotic times. Like most leaders, he wanted results and did not want to hear excuses. The problem is, few people know how to overcome their self-imposed excuses. Therefore, excuses constantly win the battle and always the war. Asking "what happened?" can only illuminate an elaborate story filled with more excuses and drama. Asking "What is the problem?" never points to the excuse. Trying to pin down "Who is responsible?" becomes a finger-pointing exercise as to who roars the loudest. These three questions complicate everything. Each eventually leads to leaders or worse employees asking the "why?" question. Asking why shows insecurity, an amateur mindset and skill set, and will lock a team into an emotional rollercoaster of despair.

As you consider your own life and the people around you and what is stopping you and the people in your life from great achievement, consider the destructive nature of asking why? without having completed the 21-day excuses challenge:

—Why is it raining outside? Now you can use the rain as an excuse.

—Why does this have to be so difficult? Now you can use difficulty as an excuse.

—Why are you yelling at me? Now you can use being yelled at as an excuse to quit or leave.

—Why am I so fat or overweight? Now you can use fat as an excuse to not work out or to just sit and eat more.

—Why does this keep happening to me? Now you can excuse yourself from having to be responsible to changing the activity that keeps happening.

—Why can't I seem to get over the hump? Now you can use the excuse of weakness, tired, painful, and exhaustion.

—Why does my knee or hip or back or shoulder hurt? Now you can excuse yourself from being responsible for that pain and learning how to adjust and deal with it.

The list of whys could go on and on for years. The why questions stop at the end of the 21-day challenge. You will *know* why because you said so or you quit: that is why. Once you realize this, you have empathy for everyone immediately and you ask the questions "How are you doing? How can I help?"

You know how they are doing. It is hard and painful and tiring. Excuses are the battle each person is in, and empathy brings out the excuses. That means you and your team can actually begin to discuss the three simple things that need to be done. The key is the evolve away from the cover-up of excuses and carve out the nonnegotiable baseline of a six-hour day of three simple things in five areas of each employee's life.

The Method:

—*Thirty minutes spiritual time (move all joints and muscles, turn on all five senses, read each of the five formulas)*

—*Ninety minutes physical time (60 minutes of primary activity, 20 minutes of stretching, drink 10 glasses of water)*

—*Thirty minutes relationship time (listen to partner, speak to partner, touch or be intimate)*

—*Thirty minutes intellectual time (learn one thing new, improve an old skill, consider "aha!" moments or epiphanies or insights)*

—*Three-hour wealth time (one hour new business, one hour existing business, one hour strategic options)*

CHAPTER EIGHT

The Method of Mentorship

The Process: Establish the difference between mentorship or management.

Acknowledgement of Purpose!

At this point in sharing both the successes and failures of a life spent serving my country, protecting my family, and applying the most difficult process of mastering my five pyramids of human performance, I ask your patience to speak some fundamental truths and untruths. The drive to pass on the process to thrive in the chaos of life comes from recent events and, perhaps, in your life as well. The world I grew up in, the world of war and killing and death, is over for me, but many of my brothers in the SEAL teams, like many in the military, remain stuck in that darkness. Sadly, I found myself unaware of the suicides and broken lives my brothers were leading for the simple reason that I had moved on and was busy raising my family and living a new life. As a point of fact, I reached out to two of my brothers who I had operated with in war and quickly realized they had succumbed to the darkness and had ended this precious life.

In the SEAL teams, on a daily basis, we all openly shared every way to lead and new skills that profoundly affected both tactics and our team's success. No one kept a secret or process from the brotherhood.

After retiring, I now openly admit that I held on to my newly discovered success, not wanting someone to take it from me. I had broken my bond of team success over individual success.

While discussing the process and method of three simple things with two of my clients who had used the training and succeeded in each of the five pyramids in their respective lives, they both suggested I write down the entire step-by-step method and share it to produce the greatest impact for the most people. Brock Barnes, the greatest success story of all, quietly said, "If you die, it dies with you!"

Mentorship or Management

The formula and the three simple things to do on a daily basis remain basic data points in a world filled with billions of data points. Like most data points, each lack context and are difficult to incorporate into a preexisting system without a guide. Three forms of incorporation exist in the world we live in: self-guided, mentor guided, manager guided. Self-guided incorporation of any skill leads to bitterness, resentment, and ineffectual use. So I will not discuss that method.

While learning to use the formula, you will first have to take responsibility for your own success. You will have to achieve personal results in each pyramid, from physical to intellectual to wealth. To achieve results in relationship and spiritual, you will have to be accountable to the results of others. Rest assured, personal results are much easier to accomplish than are the results of other people, yet the use of the formula works just the same.

Mentorship is a different animal all together. The two platforms of mentorship are full incorporation and inspiration. Mentoring someone else to use the formula and three simple things means you must test and evaluate the three simple things by incorporating each into a day of your life. In effect, to be a mentor, you will have to fully incorporate your mentees with three simple things in your life to see if they are effective.

The second aspect of mentoring is inspiration. The person you mentor must move you and inspire you. You must not see them as a problem to fix. Few people have the ability to view the world through the lens of inspiration and be moved by what they see around them. Great mentorship requires you to see the people around you as great, beautiful, inspiring, and worthy of greatness even when they don't often present that way of being.

Alas, the opposite is more the case. The case where, for example, everyone is seen as fat or unfit or everyone is dumb or unlearned or everyone is viewed as incompetent, and you are the solution to overcome his or her problems and you need to manage them. Management or developmental style leadership works in the short run, clearly. But developmental style leadership will destroy the leader and stymie the people being managed over time if that is the only method of engagement.

Let's just discuss mentorship. Mentors see greatness in you before you even know it is there. Mentors also demand greatness before you are capable of delivering even the basic level of what is being asked of you. Mentors require simplicity when all you see is the complexity of what is needed. Finally, mentors allow you to fail and feel pain and allow you to break down. Mentors embrace the difficult long-term efforts that are required to succeed.

The most difficult aspect of mentorship will always be the fact that mentors have to also continue to master their own five pyramids amidst the process of mentoring others. The foundation for mastering mentorship is to completely be responsible for personal success every day. You must model your own success if you ever expect others to demonstrate success back to you.

Step One—Inspiration

The initial method of finding what inspires you is a herculean effort. Over the past 30 years of living an inspired life, I have found it quite odd to discover many people do not live this way. The primary factor in inspiration clearly is point of view.

The point of view that inspiration or passion comes from the outside world may be the most inaccurate reflection possible. The world of social media will never provide you inspiration. Searching for passion outside of your own life will cause you stress and disappointment. Waiting for someone else to turn you on or fire you up will make you old.

Sadly, the world of TV and news will depress you, and it's designed to add virtual and artificial drama to capture your attention. Seeing death and drama on TV, even though it hasn't happened to you, is depressing. Watching *Divorce Court* as a means of entertainment affects your marriage because you then see in your partner the characteristics witnessed on TV. Ironically, millions of viewers are drawn into the drama of *The Biggest Loser*, where the obese lose weight right in front of you, while you sit there eating snacks and reacting to stressors without the ability to move and reduce stress. All the while you search for inspiration coming from outside of you, you miss the true aspect of inspiration. Passion and inspiration arise from inside of you and no other place. You must fire yourself up by your own actions and own your life. Without that truth being realized, you will follow drama and conflict and be constantly manipulated.

In order to find inspiration, look within! One simple, but not easy method to find what inspires you is to answer the following questions per pyramid. One in 10 people can honestly answer these questions because they cannot deal with truth when the virtual world allows them to experience events differently.

Physical

1. What did you do to overcome a weak muscle or difficult exercise?

2. How long did it take you to accomplish a goal?

3. What emotional responses did you have from loss or losing?

Intellectual

1. How many times or hours did it take you to learn a difficult subject?

2. What changed for you once you learned and could apply in a meaningful way what you had learned?

3. What was it like for you to have support while learning?

Wealth

1. Have you ever had no money? If so, did you find a way to make it out of the hole?

2. How long did it take you to get the job or win the contract or achieve your first big goal?

3. How many days did you just want to walk away?

Relationship

1. Have you loved someone and been rejected and found another to love as intensely?

2. How long does it take to raise a child?

3. How does it make you feel to when your spouse, lover, or family fails at an endeavor?

Spiritual

1. Does it matter to you when you hear about someone you have never met succeed in his or her life?

2. Do you pray or meditate?

3. Have you ever had an epiphany?

Each answer shows an action you must take or can take to achieve success. Or, most commonly, if your answer causes depression or drama, then you will not be capable of mentoring someone else.

Clearly overcoming personal difficulty forms the backbone of mentorship. In each question resides the experiences a mentor must have already had in his or her life. The ability to mentor literally arises from the ashes of personal failures and successes. Management doesn't require personal experiences to effectively manage people. Managers truly do not have to have overcome failure in the category to which they manage.

Managers are vital to organizations and teams. Managers are brought in to solve a particular problem or manage a specific program. They deliver a predetermined result. They produce short-term results. Managers should only be on the team for two years or less, because they will stunt inspiration and growth of the individual and organization.

Mentors are what I call "x-factors." Mentors often break things and disrupt everything to create quantum leaps in outcomes. They deliver outcomes when success was considered impossible.

Step Two—Acknowledgement

Once you establish your own inspiration and learn to see greatness in others, you then take the bold and scary step to acknowledge the other person. You literally have to tell them they inspire you. The most difficult aspect of teaching mentorship remains the act of real acknowledgement. I suppose the act of telling someone they did well or look great or telling someone they moved you to tears is frightening? Might be why few want to mentor others because the fear of rejection toward enthusiasm?

I invite you to practice acknowledgement. If you are inspired by someone in the physical pyramid, practice going up to him or her and acknowledging him or her specifically. If you are at a gym and someone does something that moves you, take the time to tell them. If someone looks great, tell them. Note what inspiration feels like for you to acknowledge someone. The feeling will surprise you.

Over the past three years of training mentors, the first two steps of mentorship have become the steps most clients have constructed a series of excuses around, thus making the steps impossible to do.

Being inspired and engaging people when you are inspired clearly is a weak muscle and needs tons of exercise. Maybe it is weak because few are inspired? Maybe inspired engagement is a weak muscle because of the lack of exercise? Either way you must constantly live inspired and acknowledge others who inspire you.

When I realized few of my clients led their lives with inspiration and rarely engaged others through the filter of inspiration, I had to develop a simple method to teach how to be inspired and engage people. And the process of inspiration works in each pyramid.

The first part of the process is to answer the questions listed above for each of the five pyramids. The second part is to engage two new people every day by simply acknowledging him or her specifically on a point of performance they demonstrated to you. You have to acknowledge two new people a day for 21 days. If you cannot complete this 21-day challenge, you cannot mentor someone else.

Step Three—Goal Driven

The next step is easy. Ask the person who inspires you what they are committed to achieving in the next two months. True mentorship begins when you align your inspiration and experience with a goal that can be measured and one that is scary for the person you mentor. Too much time and energy are wasted trying to convince your mentee to pick another goal. Too much drama and destruction are added when you cannot consistently add your inspiration and your experience to a mentee.

Sign a contract with them, where you will use all your experience and help them win! No verbal agreements will work here as a mentor. Literally sign a piece of paper articulating what you will do, what he or she will do, in order to deliver on the goal. The only difficulty here in step three is you. You, as a mentor, cannot chose their goal for them. They must select their own goal.

I have had to coach my mentor clients on the distinction of not pushing a client in the direction you want them to go but encouraging each to letting the client make the selection on their own. The reality of mentorship is to help them live their life, not to push them in a direction you perceive would make them better or happier. You have to see greatness in the person you mentor, then they must explore their own greatness.

Step Four—Detailed Plans

The old cliché "You can lead a horse to water, but you cannot make him drink" is transposed while mentoring. As a point of clarity, the reference is simply "The horse leads you to water, and you make them drink."

For a moment I ask you to consider the shift caused by allowing the client to direct the actions and ideas. Your job is to encourage the mentee to write the script, design the tactics or, rather, sketch out the plan. Clearly, you could lay out the road map to success and avoid all the pitfalls along the way. Most people are prone to telling others what to do and how to do it. Yet that is management; it will get results in the short run but will always fail in the long run when you leave the team or when you lose inspiration. Managers are solution providers and very important when an organization lacks a solution. However, recognize that once the solution is provided, the manager must exit or they will cause problems.

Instead, you must allow the mentee to stretch, to break down, to stumble, to lose heart, and to learn. Now you see why inspiration is the vital link between you and the mentee. Your job is to keep them in the fight. Their job is to do the fighting. Mentoring the person to drink, as suggested, is predicate to your experience in a giving situation. Keep encouraging them to "drink the water," because they will be prone to not doing what they had agreed to do. Take, for example, if you are a runner and your client wants to run a marathon. Don't get all entangled in which training plan is effective and which is not. Let each client design the plan. In all honesty, just download any plan from an internet search. All the plans will work if you actually do what the plan tells you to do. The difficulty will be forcing them to run and eat correctly and get sleep and stretch. You must simply keep them on task, because you know honoring your word and never giving up is the reality behind success.

Ownership of the Results

The best example I can provide comes from my friend Tim Flanagan. A true inspiration to me in each pyramid of performance. I remain inspired by Tim to this very day because of his willingness to struggle and his love for the people in his organization.

Tim leads a very successful sales organization. He contacted me directly to teach him the process and methods surrounding the five pyramids of performance and three simple things. For Tim, the entire training required a 13-month period of time. The end result, which has remained the result metric for every client, was 2X improvement in each of the five pyramids. He initially considered a 2X improvement in revenue and at work impossible. And he could not imagine that level of improvement in relationship.

He changed his mind in short order when we proved the process and method out in his physical experience of success. In short, Tim went from not running to completing a half marathon and consistently competing in Spartan races each quarter. Tim grew his business by twice the staff and twice the revenue. Most importantly, Tim used the formula of relationship to design a measurable outcome with his wife and together they cultivated the 2X lifestyle.

More to the point, I wanted to share the process of mentoring that was done within the system of using the formula and three simple things to achieve the 2X lifestyle. Results are fun to look at and discuss! Yet results are always dependent on three simple things as well.

Tim had the willingness and capacity to learn the formula. The formula applied over time works every time. And I had to fully immerse myself and mentor until the completed goals stood proudly on his wall. To mentor successfully, you need the mentee, the process and methods, and the mentor. Three simple things of mentorship are disturbingly difficult to establish!

The secret I have never shared regarding the method of mentorship to produce 2X results will be the toughest to absorb into your practice. The secret of success rests solely on the ability of the mentor to incorporate the exact three simple things the mentee will be doing each day into his or her life. The mentor must practice what the mentee is doing to resolve the effectiveness. You must own the entire formula you are asking the mentee to use. If they select swimming, then I had to do the swim workout. If they select a new way to prospect a client, I had to use that way as well.

With Tim, I also had to use what he suggested as a workout plan to prepare for the half marathon. I had to spend a day with Tim pursuing the plan to grow his business. And, finally, I had to incorporate Tim's relationship activities into my activities with my wife.

The ownership process of mentoring described comes from the proven experiences passed down from the Navy SEAL community from the combat lessons of leading men ranging from the scouts and raiders in World War Two to Vietnam to Afghanistan and Iraq. The clear distinction between management and mentorship remains evident in the SEAL community and works rather well in business. In the SEAL teams, leaders manage the men who are in battle, and SEAL chiefs mentor men in chaos by the method of demonstrate, observe, and incorporate techniques. Managers and leaders are critical to strategy and oversight. But leading during chaos comes from mentors with patience and experience, people actually dive into the tactics and actions with the men in the battle. Only the ones willing to incorporate the changes and prove the changes out win the war.

Tim's three simple things to complete a half marathon began at 5:30 a.m. with an hour run. The next thing we discussed with much debate involved retaining a flexibility trainer to spend 20 minutes at 5:30 p.m. with Tim to teach and ensure stretching. Throughout the day he promised to drink 10 full glasses of water. Tim and I signed the contract to engage in the marathon training for 21 days. He was responsible for those three simple things for 21 days. I was responsible for calling once a week for three weeks. My job as a mentor was to first incorporate Tim's three simple things into one of my days to see how the actions would affect me.

The same process proved effective with wealth and relationship. During the first phone call, I had experienced what it was like to be Tim and engage in the three simple things he had agreed to doing. The saying "If you want to know someone, walk a day in their shoes" works really well. Early morning workouts are effective but have a pitfall I had experienced both as a SEAL and by incorporating Tim's day into mine. Early morning workouts make you sore in the first week, energized in the second week, and make you impatient with others who don't work out in the third week. Early morning workouts also cause relationship conflicts because the one working out wakes up the spouse and is out of the house until later that evening. I knew this would begin to strain the relationship, because the truth is that it strained mine. The loneliness of always working out in the morning is what I have learned to reference as "the death of a thousand cuts in a relationship."

By incorporating your mentee's three simple things into your life for a day, you develop a reference of reality to discuss. Mutual experiences are vital to leading during chaos. As a mentor you also learn new aspects regarding old habits or old skill sets. My notebook for mentoring Tim had pages of experiences and pages of questions and suggestions. No matter what my opinion had evolved into or devolved away from, I could not hint or suggest his three simple things were wrong or bad in any way. Even if Tim was in pain or exhausted or sick, I, as his mentor, could not suggest he abandon his actions and dishonor his word. You will destroy the people in your life if you let them constantly excuse themselves from doing what they said they would do for any reason. Trust me on this point, listening to drama and excuses and giving your mentee a break will destroy them and in turn destroy your life in the same area.

Mentors must commit and see the whole effort through . . . even when the mentee has breakdowns and conflicts. All adaptations and changes can only come from the mentee.

The original 21-day challenge of relationship, physical, and wealth took Tim 69 days to complete. Pain and spousal support caused several restarts during the first 7 days. Once through the 7-day effort, the final two weeks became habit and easy. Every single client in the past 6 years fails either in the first 7 days or in the last 2 days. Pain and lack of support and "I forgot" used as excuses are the killers of success. The phrase "this is stupid" kills clients seeking real wealth and success in the final 2 days. Tim showed signs of failing in the final 2 days, and during a 2-hour meeting we reset the value of honoring your word and never giving up. The 21-day challenge, once complete, built the foundation for the 2X success metric Tim gained later.

Even though Tim experienced several bumps during the initial work, the greatest advantage of incorporating the mentorship practice came from the day I spent mirroring him in the wealth pyramid. Successful men and women develop a routine. And without a routine, success in any endeavor might not be possible. The big issue in long-term success for all leaders rests in the simple human failing that routines become blind spots for efficiencies and emotionally charged activities that can no longer be altered from the inside. In short, Tim succeeds by routinely addressing his day, and he did not realize the routine was no longer effective.

Our agreement focused on achieving a baseline of three simple things each day. I looked for one hour of prospecting for either new clients or new hires. I tried to discern from the noise of his day at least one hour of nurturing and caring for existing clients and employees. Finally, my task of helping flesh out at least one hour of strategic, unrestricted thinking of the future relied heavily on determining if Tim could break away from dealing with his business to create a space for the future.

Being a SEAL chief with multiple combat tours exposed me not only to how horrific war is but also to how great the human condition truly is during chaos. I remain awestruck how the original SEALs, such as Draper Kaufman and the men who wrote the SEAL training curriculum, broke from tradition and demanded SEAL leaders and chiefs to demonstrate proficiency and lead during chaos with the men. They ingrained the condition of mentorship and immersion and incorporating the tactical decisions into their own lives. The unique aspect of the incorporated mentor comes from actually witnessing reality from the point in time when actions are happening. Literally, you have to be there to make a choice and that choice made from the front lines is vastly different than the one made from the safety of a command center.

Had I not been fully incorporated into Tim's day, I would have missed the facts. Tim had missed the facts himself. During our end of day brief, I asked if he had accomplished his three simple things and his reply was absolutely. In fact, he had not. Like most business owners who build a business from the ground up, he had constructed the structured business around personal interactions with his employees. Tim is an empathic leader and a great teacher of skill sets. Tim had 13 direct reports in a company with 300 employees scattered between four cities. Each day he spent 12 hours attempting to engage them all in meaningful ways. During our day together, I realized he had no nonnegotiable baseline. Tim, like so many others, was a master at adjusting and dealing with the crisis of the moment. Crisis management works in the short run. Tim negotiates very effectively with whatever comes his way.

Crisis management literally is defensive operations and is only one of the three simple things. Point in fact, Tim spent 10 hours dealing with the crisis of existing clients and employees. Even his notional new client time centered around trying to hire someone new because an existing employee had not had enough Tim time and was losing heart. As you can now realize, even in the strategic meeting he did have, it was more dealing with existing issues than unconstrained dialogue about where they wanted to go in five years.

As you mature at the practice of mentorship and three simple things, you will realize most issues surrounding wealth and growth in organizations are not product, sales techniques, or even location. Most issues that compromise an organization are centered around egos or people. The egos of leaders and employees. Egos cause blind spots and emotional commitments to actions within an organization that make no impact to the company or people. You, as a mentor, have to see these egos and know what to do.

"Tim," I said, pausing after hearing him say he hit the mark, "what is it like to have to deal with 13 direct reports?"

"It is my responsibility to keep them all abreast of my vision and the mission of the organization as well as address what issues they may have," he answered rather matter-of-factly. "Ours is a business of relationships both internal and external!"

"You do seem to enjoy nurturing each relationship, that point is clear," I told Tim, while redirecting to the not so obvious ego point. "Let me make a straightforward observation. One which is a leader's capacity to effectively engage others. Humans, and in your case, leaders, can effectively only engage three people a day. Most leaders realize this fact and create three direct reports who are critical to engage every single day. These direct reports are responsible for new business, existing business, and strategic initiatives. Who are these three people," I asked. "Can I see your organizational chart?"

Mentorship through deep involvement always exposes what I call "stuff." Stuff that is hidden and covered up and often emotionally charged with disturbing conversations regarding why a particular person or process exists. As a mentor you will know of the cover-up of stuff because when you incorporate the three simple things into your life, you will see that you actually cover up and hide the same issues.

The great part of mentorship is that you will not be ego centered nor emotionally involved in the hiding of the stuff.

As Tim detailed his organizational chart and who each person was and their level of responsibilities, he stopped and noted how convoluted the chart was. He stopped the ego. Every leader will notice the ego and the cover-up if you don't make them wrong or make them fight to explain. All ego is a cover-up of feelings of personal inadequacy or a cover-up of someone else's shortcomings. Great mentors take the opposite to an ego-driven approach. Great mentors want to expose what is not working so that a solution to make it work can arise. Every problem has a solution. Ego perpetuates problems. Especially when the solution may be the removal of a person within an organization to which the leader may have a personal attachment to retaining.

"Tim, the question is who within your direct reports isn't effective and who isn't working for you on a personal note?" I asked.

"Two people aren't," he replied. And he spelled out both what wasn't effective in their actions and the emotional conflict he had each night after work while trying to come up with ways to resolve each ineffective action.

"Your three direct reports need to be set up, and each of them need to be producing effective actions and have no emotionally retained baggage. Three simple things for you as a leader could be rephrased as three simple people. All your other daily activities are used to compensate for you not having these three simple things, or people, as the nonnegotiable baseline use of your time and your energy," I said. "Each day you need to spend an hour with each of your three categoric people: your offensive or new client facing, your operations or existing businessperson, and either you alone or you with someone who is unencumbered with the day-to-day dealings to think strategically.

"Can we reset the 21-day challenge to set up a baseline of three hours of your time with these direct reports?" I asked. "During the next 21 days, you will resolve a great many issues. Obviously, after those three hours are complete, engage with anyone you want. My promise to you is, after 21 days all the ego and emotion and ineffective actions will be resolved."

Sixty-nine days later Tim became a healthy and rather good runner. He communicated effectively with his spouse that led to mutual support and excitement I rarely see in couples married over 10 years or more. Most importantly, Tim gave more time to his direct reports and created a plan for the next five years that had the support of his people and detailed opportunities each quarter.

As a mentor, on day 70 after we began the process, my life too had a new level of clarity and actionable items because I had learned new skills about my own health and relationship and business practices by incorporating Tim's plan into my own life.

During the 69-day mentorship, however, and this point may be the most important point of mentorship that scares people toward management only, my own five pyramids of performance and achievements struggled to produce results. The practice of mentoring another person toward his or her own successes always causes temporary stagnation in the mentor's own success. The phenomenon is real for me each time, yet the day after the mentee succeeds, my own five pyramids take a leap forward with new skills and new tactics. Mentoring always adds measurable value to both the mentor and the mentee but requires temporarily loss for the mentor.

The choice to mentor or to manage is entirely up to you. Management is always a temporary upside, much like taking a drug. Mentoring is always a temporary slowing for personal results, then a much bigger upside in the long run. Play the long game of mentorship!

The Method: Mentorship includes inspiration, acknowledgement, measurable goals, detail plans, and ownership of the results. Must mentor one person per pyramid every three months.

A Personal Note from Tim Flanagan

"As I share the story of how Thom and I met, I point out our meeting was divinely inspired. I had just completed Thom's book *Unbreakable: A Navy SEAL's Way of Life* and had resolved to meet him in order to learn more about who he was and how his training might help me in my life. Within two hours of making this declaration, a mutual acquaintance reached out to introduce us, without any prompting or request from me.

"Our first meeting led to me asking Thom to train and mentor me using the principles from his book. Thom is an intense and unique individual. I was intrigued by what I could learn from Thom and how I could integrate his training and experience as a SEAL into my business. Little did I know that I was setting my life on a course to learn how to fully realize my potential in all areas of my life.

"On January 28, 2011, I suffered a significant injury in a skiing accident and completely shattered my left tibia plateau and broke my fibula. The injury required that my tibia plateau be replaced with one from a cadaver in a complicated surgery. My surgeon had informed me my days of running and skiing, as well as anything physical, had come to an end, at 44 years of age. I accepted this fate and adjusted my life accordingly. My wife and I running and skiing together had come to an end. I harbored feeling of frustration and regret as well as a sense of brokenness.

"Thom and I met early in the creation of his training and mentoring program. The first cycle was working in what he calls the physical pyramid. I admired the fact that Thom did Ultra races and also shared with him my earlier life as runner but couldn't continue due to my leg injury. His answer, 'Runners run,' disturbed me. I tried unsuccessfully to explain my situation to him, his answer was, 'Runners run.' What I did next was not his prompting, and my doctor definitely would not have approved, but I decided to run. The next Saturday morning I begrudgingly got on a treadmill and ran three miles. The experience brought me to tears, not because it hurt, that came later, but because

I could do it. My enthusiasm had overcome my excuses and had me running again. Sunday, I ran another five miles. Wow, runners run is simple, and I had learned Thom's first lesson of defeating excuses and reasons. To be fair, my legs fell apart and I spent two months after those eight miles back in rehab, which I had quit the first time.

"Thom shared with me I needed a big scary goal and a team and plan to accomplish that goal. I decided to do the Charlotte Half Marathon in November 2015, with Thom. The fact he always insisted he participate in each of my goals further disturbed me. Something I thought would never be possible had become very real: even my surgeon agreed it was safe. Working in this pyramid opened up a whole new world to me physically, and I have since become a regular Spartan racer earning two Trifectas and running in Spartan races every three months.

"The training had really just begun. Being a slow learner and what I had thought a very busy man seemed to cause the training to slowly progress over an entire year. I can say the work we did in all five pyramids was nothing short of remarkable. Together we achieved twice as much as I had originally intended.

"In relationship, we worked on my marriage. Without revealing too much personal information and respecting that my wife is a very private person, I can say that the training set my marriage on a much more positive and intimate path. I had been completely unaware how far off I had gotten in supporting my wife until the training. We have been married 30 years now, and we are in the best place we have ever been. I directly attribute that to one conversation I had with Thom during our training. One question changed the entire direction of my marriage and the courage I had to have to ask that question to my wife. I learned to support my wife's life and not ask her to give up her life for mine.

"In my business life, we had been presented with some significant opportunities while in training with Thom. Again, working within process and methods of formula for human performance, we were able to not only pursue that opportunity, but others, and have doubled a rather large company by a factor of 2X in four years.

"Working in the spiritual pyramid also opened up rich connection in my life and a sense of peace that I had not known before. My faith has always been important to me, and the training opened up this part of my life in ways that are difficult for me to articulate in words. The peace, presence, and focus I enjoy now are wonderful gifts. This path of the training has taken me longer to grasp and came with a real and ongoing examination of how I deal with fear and my insecurities.

"Working with Thom has been a blessing and a game changer for my health, my business, and my family. I gained much more than I thought possible. I, and I think our society, has made life very complicated. Thom's training strips the complexity out and replaces it with simplicity. That doesn't make it easy, yet simplicity is much more likely to be executed successfully over any complexity. Life is about execution, what you do, and who you are as you live each day. Not what you say you will do, or hope you will do, but what you actually do."

CHAPTER NINE

Never Give up on YOU

The Process: Determine what is required when
"things" don't go as planned.

"I had read Thom's book Unbreakable: A Navy SEAL's Way of Life *and was inspired at how he had a strong woman in his life during his career as a Navy SEAL and throughout several wartime deployments. I wanted to learn how to be that woman." ~Noel, 2015*

In this chapter I am going to share the story of Noel, a 47-year old woman I trained. Why? I want to show you that the three simple things for each of the five pyramids are nonnegotiable and have a great impact on having a great life. The circumstances of each of our lives will most assuredly cause pain and cause you to change your dreams. And you may give up and have to start again, like Noel did. Noel and I taught each other!

Every single client I train changes me. Although this change is rarely expressed to the client, the long process of mentoring and incorporating the different action items clients consider to be successful into my life often brings about the same breakdowns the client experiences. Thank God for Hell Week!

By the time I met Noel, my mentoring business had grown to a robust practice. I traveled three to four days a week, training eight clients a month across the country. All of the clients were already successful male, business owners who simply had overworked their businesses and had neglected health and relationship. The rhythm and issues became comfortable to address and predictable. I had four clients waiting to begin training, because I knew from a life in the SEAL teams not to take on more work than you can actually deliver in the expressed value you promised.

Something about the multiple emails and the many phone calls piqued my interest to begin training Noel. Her expressed commitment to her children and her excitement regarding the work she did as a saleswoman set her in a different place in my thoughts than most clients. During the big phone call where we agreed to start the training that would surely take a year (or more), I asked the simple question about being a "Spartan Woman" most people don't expect.

"Noel, I like your excitement to want to be like Stacy and you reading *Unbreakable* always makes me happy to hear, but let me try to talk you out of it," I said.

"What do you mean talk me out of it? I admire the way you talk about Stacy and your love for her. I want that in my life," she said.

"Because you have to give up being right and give up being subservient. A Spartan woman never compromises her strength for a man's weakness. She knows if the relationship is going to last very long, it is not up to the man and how he treats her. The opposite is the real truth. She has to be strong when he is weak. Women often want a great relationship but don't want to be responsible to their strength and comprise themselves too often. Men suck without a strong woman. If your man sucks, it is because of you. So do you still want to begin training?" I fully expected Noel to hang up.

"Yes, I am enthused and crave learning about that Spartan woman life," she stated.

As we agreed to begin, and I looked at my phone and pressed "end call" on the screen, a level of discomfort came over me. Reflecting on the level of openness and private conversations that come up during training with men, I wondered if I could deal with the sharing a woman would have. Worse than that, I had not considered how uncomfortable Stacy might be with me traveling to train Noel. The only way to be responsible to all factors was to have Stacy and Noel discuss the training and outcomes prior to actually beginning.

At this point I want to share with you the hard truth: Men rarely offer their wives the "chairman" seat of their businesses or in any aspect of their lives. If you are a male reader cringing at the idea, then you will never know great success. If you are a woman celebrating, just remember you have to give up being weak and subservient.

When I approached Stacy with my concerns and request for her to engage Noel, I stumbled a bit. Stacy listened to my concerns and noticed my body language was considerably different than normal.

"Good Lord, why are you acting like a child?" she asked. "Are you afraid of training a woman? Don't be concerned what I think about you sitting in a room with a woman all day. Don't worry about what other people may think either. This is our business to transform people. I don't understand why Noel is any different for you."

"I don't know that I am scared," I said, pausing to consider. "I first wanted you to know I was going to train a woman. And secondly, I wanted you involved."

"No, you are scared!" she said. "What about training a woman makes you this way?" she asked.

It took me a moment to come to terms with what she was seeing in my reaction. "It isn't fear or being scared. I am uncomfortable with the possibility of listening to excuses and complaints all day. With men, I can just shut them down and tell them to stop complaining. In my mind, women tend to blame others and circumstances and have soft skin when smacked with truth," I replied.

"Well, get off of it and stop treating other women as if they are weak. You don't treat me that way. I will call Noel if you want me to, but you have got to treat everyone as if they are bold and as if they are God," she said.

The problem with strong women is when you allow one in your life, they make weakness so uncomfortable. I stood there as she walked away, wondering what had just happened. I wondered how a simple question of calling Noel had exposed my level of discomfort. The statement to treat everyone as if they are God struck me as a great mindset to have in all aspects of life. I couldn't be a wimp in front of God, that is clear.

Exposing Excitement

The first day of training begins the evolutionary process to expose the clients to the principles to honor your word and never give up and establish the formula. The day is rather long in duration for two reasons. The first reason is the material is extensive and has to be covered to set up the difficult work each client has to complete after the first day. The second reason is, until exhaustion happens, the client isn't in a state to learn something powerful. The latter reason remains the key factor to what stops people in general from learning something new: people always use their energy to protect the status quo.

Evolution One, as I call it, normally exhausts me completely. I recall the first time I trained a client, I literally had to take a nap in my truck in the parking lot. This fact disturbed me because I viewed myself as tough, well able to handle long hours of work. The intensity of the day requires complete attention to both what I am saying and what the client is hearing. The constant pressure to ensure the material is completely absorbed demands repetition, rephrasing, and often emotional breakdowns. For me it requires all of my energy and for me to not get stuck emotionally on anything. The day with Noel seemed not to exhaust either of us.

When excitement occurs, learning is simple and application, too, is simple. Noel brought a level of excitement to the training I find as a rare element. She was just genuinely excited. Most of us are often reserved, guarded, and worse, resigned and cynical. The older I get, the more I realize how cynical I also am. Yet the battle between excitement and cynicism normally happens during Evolution One, which causes the overall drain.

I found the entire experience to be odd. Odd in the fact that she had little to be excited about, from my perspective. Yes, she had two awesome children, yet she was divorced and had no respect for the ex-husband. Noel worked hard and had to balance work and family, and I could tell the daily grind frustrated her, and she felt alone. She explained her passion for health yet had no time to have big, scary, audacious goals in the physical space. She had a great house in the settlement and some inheritance and knew she couldn't sustain their lifestyle. The paradox of being excited, even though her life was not the one she wanted, was stunning to witness. Anyone who can gener-ate excitement in a swamp filled with leeches and mosquitoes cannot be beaten.

Evolution One and the 21-day homework challenge are literally de-signed to create a foundation of three simple things to enable the client to be excited every day about activity. The foundation of sustainable success is to do simple activity every single day, whether the world you live in is going according to plan or is erupting. I knew if Noel brought self-generated excitement, the three simple things design would help her create the life she wanted for herself and her daughters. The old cliché that everything dies in execution literally means without excite-ment and without doing simple actions, then no great dream has any chance of being realized.

Exposing the Weak Points

The 21-day challenge to do three simple things a day exposes many weak points. Obviously, the weak points we previously discussed are exposing excuses and exposing the activities that may be hard to do. From the client's point of view, those two points are of great value. From my point of view, the weak points that become evident are the previous daily structure of activities and external influences which are perpetuating lack of success. In other words, I had to find ways to help Noel continue to be excited as we exposed the people in her life who aren't helping and the previous activities that are destroying her success.

I was very concerned with her excitement. She had structured her morning and night around her daughters. Noel had also talked herself into conducting her physical workout during the day, prior to picking up her daughters. As a mentor, I too would have to incorporate her plan into my day to determine the advantages and disadvantages for me. I further knew any method of completing three simple things is better than talking yourself out of even doing them. Yet as we both began the 21-day challenge, we both immediately discovered the weakness.

For a moment, I ask your patience to discuss the categories of weak points I look for. Physical weaknesses are the easiest to determine and the easiest to make stronger. The most immediate impact to every single person is to get stronger, obtain more endurance, and ultimately feel fitter. Often, when you expose a physical weakness, the weakness is actually something they want to make stronger.

The second weakness I look for is the emotional attachment people have to a choice they have previously made. This weakness is both difficult to see and even more difficult to transform. Waiting for the list of excuses while watching the struggle is always the fun part of training. Knowing when to confront the excuse and how far down you allow the client to fall is not the fun part of training, because falling kills excitement. I did not want Noel to lose excitement.

The third weakness, which creates the biggest conflict, is when the people in the client's life who are not helpful get exposed. No one wants to see the people they have in their life as not beneficial, and worse, as harmful. And imagine what you would notice about your own choices when you realize you surround yourself with harmful people. Noticing you actually pick the wrong people is difficult for most people to realize.

The three weak points are critical to expose without destroying excitement to engage in three simple things. Pain and physical weaknesses have to be exposed, a plan to overcome them must be engaged. Ego and emotional attachment to bad choices must be brought to the surface very quickly, and the only way to overcome a destructive ego is to let go of being right. Finally, a softer hand is needed when harmful people are identified. The primary five people you spend the most time with each day have to be committed to you. I find this weakness the most challenging to expose and to transform. I knew Noel had people in her day-to-day life who were negative and would have to be dealt with to allow her to actually do the three simple things.

The excuses and reasons, again, reflect what most people honor. Noel communicated her excuses like she was a professional saleswoman. The first excuse that became apparent in doing the 21-day challenge, to carve out the spiritual, physical time and three simple things, was pain and difficulty. All new actions are painful. Doing push-ups in the morning and at night hurt even if you are an athlete. The actions either hurt your body or they disrupt your preexisting routine, which is painful. Pain is easy to deal with by just slowing down and engaging in spite of how you feel.

The excuses around ego and emotion strike a different chord. Emotional attachments cannot easily be pushed aside to do simple actions. Every single emotional attachment is heard as an excuse I call "this is stupid." Every time you hear yourself or someone else say "this is stupid" is because of ego or an emotional attachment. Yet ego and emotion prevent the action you had agreed to doing from being done. Noel at first excused herself from doing the three simple things during the day because she said, "This is stupid.

"Thom, I didn't work out on Wednesday because I didn't have time. And, on Thursday, I didn't want to get sweaty before school pickups," she said to convince me. "Noel, excuses to not do what you have promised are subtle, seductive, and believable. They always make sense, don't they," I said, pushing back gently.

"I didn't have the time because midday I got a call from a friend who had a crisis and I didn't want to abandon her," she said, layering on the believability. "I don't like to pick up my daughters soaked with sweat. It is irresponsible mothering."

"Noel, the training isn't about right and wrong. I simply want you to experience the dynamic between honoring your word or honoring your excuse and the impact what you honor has on what you do. My question back to you is did you do what you promised you would do?" I asked.

"No, I didn't. I just didn't organize my day correctly. If I change how I organize my day, it will be easier," she professed.

"Noel, the issue isn't being organized at all. The more powerful way to look at attaining the goal is honoring your work and breaking the complexity of your day to three simple, nonnegotiable actions. Either the actions have value, or they do not. At this point you are showing me and telling yourself the actions have no value and your word or promise has zero impact on what you do. Possibly you are emotionally attached to how you feel and your opinion than you are regarding succeeding. Can you tell me what you were feeling when you broke your promise?" I asked.

"I cannot control when my friends have a crisis. I never want to abandon a friend who needs help. And, my working out seemed like a self-indulgent luxury while a friend needed a hand. Do you think that is wrong?" she asked.

"My goodness, I find working with you exciting, because you are a great communicator. I am not here to tell you right or wrong regarding anything. My opinion of right or wrong is not relevant and has no value. My opinion, actually everyone's individual opinion, is never the actions they do. Saying that another way is, people know what is right but often do what is wrong. I am only looking at what you do. My question is what did you do?" I reframed and pushed the conversation forward.

"I helped my friend instead of working out for the hour I promised," she stated.

"Facts are fun. When I myself tried to workout at 1:30 in the afternoon, because that is when you suggested you would, I also found the effort difficult because my day at that point is always dealing with crisis. Even the workout you were to do, that I also was attempting to do, was draining and difficult because the crises I had stopped dealing with were still going on and my mind wasn't interested in the workout. I, however, honored my word to you and myself. Without that, then the training we are doing has little upside and value. I would be stealing your money and just giving you more complexity," I said.

"Now, the question is, what was the emotion you were feeling that prevented you from honoring your word?" I asked.

Ego and emotion are very complex on the surface. Emotions are very practical when used as keys that open locks to predetermined outcomes. The question to always ask is this: is that the emotional response you are having and what is the predetermined outcome? Since few teachers or parents actually teach emotions and outcomes for using emotions, the human condition of big egos and emotional immaturity consistently make life complex and goals very difficult to achieve. People have inflated egos and are emotionally attached to being right instead of just doing what they said they would do.

The vulnerable interaction which transpired brought out the exact emotion. Noel and I have agreed to not discuss the details because of the involvement of other people and how out of context most of the conversations were in the scope of the interaction and the topic of egos and outcomes. After two hours the emotion she was experiencing became clear: frustration and disappointment. These are the twin emotions that cause the perpetuation of things to constantly happen again and again and again in our lives. Frustration literally causes the events which frustrate us to keep occurring, which causes more frustration and more disappointment.

Noel finally understood. "I feel frustration. I feel it because I cannot seem to get over the hump after the divorce. I feel disappointed I cannot get enough work done. I am disappointed where my life is, and I have two daughters and am not married. I am frustrated I don't have time to work out. I did not want this to happen to me," she said after a time.

"Noel, emotions are helpful or hurtful. Yet there is another possible way to move forward more powerfully, and that way is to set up actions you know are vital to your success and carving out time and energy in your day where you will do them. Until this nonnegotiable time and three simple things is set in stone, emotional effects and excuses are what you experience. I have found that the time to achieve your baseline of three simple things is best completed in the morning before you leave the house. Because life is more complex at this juncture once you are involved in the broader experience of the day. What time in the morning would you have to get up in order to accomplish the 60-minute run and exercise routine?" I asked.

"I would have to get up by 5:15," she calculated.

"Perfect. Let's begin again and adjust so that you can honor your word and succeed," I said.

The next 21 days flowed together seamlessly. Noel altered the time of day she promised to conduct the main part of her physical baseline to be early in the day. The three simple, spiritual things tied together well into the intentionality she had already established due to her previous belief system and practices. And, Noel quieted her list of excuses during the final few days in spite of the "this is stupid" excuse attempting to spoil her efforts on day 21.

The second evolution occurred without any problem. From previous client trainings, I had shifted the sequence to teach intentionality and focus instead of emotional mastery. The change allowed the client to not be bogged down in emotional turmoil but allowed what I call accuracy of action and thought to cause momentum in the three pyramids of value. In Evolution Two we scoped out the impact of focus or living "on point" and added the wealth formula to the next 21-day challenge.

Noel also demonstrated her complete ability to manage fear during the day of training by conquering the 90-foot rappel and the difficult climb back to the top. As a trainer, I recognize that classroom style training has limited value in dealing with fear and find that having to leap off a 90-foot wall and climb back up to be the only way to teach what fear does to people and how to beat it. In general, people who are locked up and afraid to leap into the rappel rationalize excuses everywhere in their lives. The experience of climbing back up always shows the people who lack balance in their life and who just push through their lives to get to the end. If you are a climber, you know the truth about resting often and planning out the next move as the most efficient way to proceed. Noel had no fear at all. And she stopped after every move up the wall to recover from muscle fatigue and plan the next step. Ironically, every woman has made the climb and only 60 percent of the men do. The reason is, fear of making a mistake causes men to charge through and burn out. Women seem not to burn out and are more methodical.

Never Negotiate Even When the Future Seems Bleak

The real value of a long training timeline is to show the true value of maintaining the baseline of three simple things whether the client is winning or losing in life. The simple truth is both are temporary. The difficult truth regarding winning and losing is that both seem to always make people forget the basics.

Winning blows up basic actions. Winning inflates ego. Winning strains relationships.

Losing makes people disregard every fundamental principle in their life. Losing causes emotional negativity. Losing destroys relationships.

With the introduction of the wealth formula, Noel's goal was to move to another state to increase her business, decrease her cost of living, and start a new life. Like most goals, success was dependent on three things: Noel not giving up, committed partners, and a detailed plan that boiled down to doing three simple things a day. Part of the plan entailed going to court to renegotiate for the out-of-state relocation pertaining to her two daughters.

Negotiation is a four-letter word in life, and I knew the implications. I look at negotiations as weak positions only used by politicians, never to be used by normal humans. "Lest we forget" that politicians negotiate poorly quite often, and war ensues. Warriors never negotiate. Yet I was excited to learn something new as a mentor regarding how life changes impact the baseline.

The resettlement proceedings were injected smack dab in the first week of the third 21-day challenge iteration. The third challenge involves maintaining the spiritual, intellectual, wealth, and physical time and three simple things; it also adds carving out time for relationship and the three simple things for relationship to be effective. The training had also added the concept of emotional mastery, and the court proceedings acted like a grenade exploding. While Noel was exposing her day-to-day world to emotions, the court drama enhanced all the emotional attachments of a previous marriage.

My form of mentorship means I too had to attempt to deal with trying to maintain the three simple things she had selected and to encounter the emotions Noel had determined to work through as well. The combination was lethal in the fact it destroyed my baseline and made me disregard my commitments and only deal with trying to figure out the court case. The emotional cesspool quickly sucked me in and even began to affect my relationship with Stacy. I knew Noel was stuffed.

For six months, Noel abandoned her baseline and just dealt with the resettlement. At the end, she lost and had to remain in the same state. During the proceedings, her health diminished, her wealth barely had any activity, and the relationship work never happened.

When negotiation is on the table, people always lose sight of three simple things.

"Noel," I said once she was in a place to rethink about training, "whether you think you are going to win or lose in life, never negotiate with who you are and your commitment to the three simple things that bring you value. Even if you had won, you stopped honoring your word to yourself."

"I was so depressed and exhausted, I couldn't find the time or energy to stay with the program, so I just decided to put off the training until the verdict came back," she stated.

"External tragedies, huge snowstorms, illnesses, election cycles, wildfires, or whatever outside events happen will always be present. They all seem so important and imminent. But external events are *you*. I think it's more important to master the skills of who you are by ensuring you maintain the nonnegotiable baseline of three simple things per pyramid every day. The baseline only takes six hours to do the activities. My question is a hard one, but I must ask it. What caused you to drop everything?" I asked.

She didn't answer, because excuses don't seem like excuses. Excuses seem to cause an immediate resetting of priority and destroy existing goals. And the transition from a directed, goal-driven life to one of negotiating with yourself to shift to a new mindset and action plan happens in a millisecond. Eventually, Noel said, "I had to do whatever I needed to do to ensure I won the case," a plea to convince me of her shift!

"You didn't have to excuse yourself from a life you have chosen. But you did. Now the time and energy required to get back on track and reaffirm you do honor your word will be harder than had you maintained your word. You cannot get back lost time and effort. I ask of you just one shift in how you look at yourself and this training." I stopped to get her attention. "I ask you to consider never negotiating with your baseline. We start again tomorrow and reset all the formulas to goals that you cannot live without. Then, begin executing on the

21-day challenge to reward or pull out the monetary value of your actions."

The most extraordinary change occurred that has altered my perception of the greatness in humans. Noel changed all her formula goals. She changed them because she said, "I want a life I cannot live without." More importantly, she expressed she wanted a man in her life she was proud of being married to and one who supported her. Stacy and I discussed how powerful a commitment like that is and what is required of both of us as mentors, and Noel as a mentee, to accomplish.

Noel would have to learn to not compromise and not negotiate. Two rather difficult character traits to relearn, especially at 47 years old. The process was simple and methods very straightforward. We were to mentor Noel to maintain her baseline of three simple things per pyramid every day. Because, in truth, unless you love yourself and have a great life, you cannot be loved by someone else who has a great life.

Within the next year, Noel completed the training, hit her fitness goals, increased her income, and got married to a powerful man who met the mark she had created. To arrive at that place of measurable success, she had to emotionally let go and give up being right. Noel had to stop using excuses to prevent her from her achievements.

Three simple things executed over time always make you arrive at your destination. That destination is "YOU!"

The Method: Rather than abandoning the formula, reset the entire process and start again.

A Personal Message from Noel

"Coaching has always been a vital ingredient to my latter adult life. In my eyes, Thom was a warrior—scary, intimidating, unrelenting—and I had never received coaching from a man. The greatest impetus, then, to seek one-on-one coaching from Thom was my vibrant young daughters, who epitomize growth outside their comfort zones. Because of wanting to perpetually model to them, I am constantly seeking ways to be a better mother, businesswoman, citizen, and wife, while uncovering avenues of growth far outside my own comfort zone. Establishing more courage is not comfortable, and my daughters bore witness to this journey firsthand. Thom and Stacy Shea led me to a firmer platform in which to 'own my space,' define what courage looks like in the face of adversity, and to honor my word to the people that matter most, myself included. The life of a Spartan woman is worth it."

CHAPTER TEN

Searching for the Alpha Wolf

The Process: Determine the value of a leader.

I break down people into four distinct groups. Making these distinctions in my mind does, however, cause many missed opportunities and many misunderstandings. People I meet immediately fall into these four groups: wolf, sheep, sheep dog, and the omega. As I describe the characteristics of each, can you identify your type?

After working with each group both in the SEAL teams and in the business and personal sectors, each group expresses and utilizes the formula the same way. The omegas however have no foundation of "honor your word" and "never give up." But they too are masters of language and use the formula without realizing it and cannot be convinced to alter even one word or action in the formula. An omega knows he or she is broken, scarce, finite, separate, and that their life has no meaning. He or she also has clear and distinct goals to prove who they are . . . just ask them. They cannot focus, they are emotionally stuck, fear change, and refuse to be mentored. The partners and social groups are fully committed to supporting the omega to continue to be an outlier. Their day-to-day actions clearly support their lifestyle. And when asked why, each omega will answer with "Because this is all that is left for me."

The sheep form the majority of the people you will encounter. Sheep band together with like-minded people who do similar things on a daily basis. As long as the group "honors the group agreements," they too will keep theirs. As long as the collective "keeps moving," so will they. The formula for human performance works well when the collective narrative fills the wording out for each person. The collective wording for sheep changes to we instead of me. We are unbreakable, abundant, infinite, one, and meaningful. Their goals are written as a group and can only be accomplished as a group. As long as the group is focused, so is the individual. The collective group determines what emotional responses are appropriate and demand each person respond the same. Each has little fear as long as the group is together yet fears leaving the collective. The partners within the group of sheep actually work rather well to support the actions of each member. Each sheep is relegated to no more than simple tasks and punishes more tasks being accomplished. Their collective answer to "why" is because "I was told to."

The final two distinct groups are very similar in their lifestyles and use of the formula. The only distinct difference is the partner section of the formula. In short, who they determine to be their partners define if they are a wolf or a sheep dog. Each "honors their word" at all costs. When a wolf or a sheep dog says it will do something, trust me it will do it. Each will die in the pursuit of his or her goals. What is fascinating is how huge their defined goals are. Both the sheep dog and wolf play on a very big scale.

A sheep dog's physical goal is to be stronger than a pack of wolves. Consider that for a second. A sheep dog has to not just defend against one wolf and other predators but also defend and defeat a pack. A sheep dog's view shifts from self-interest to defining themselves as the head of the group. The protector is laser focused even when asleep. They have little emotional reactions to the wanderings of the sheep and the protests by the sheep when they must move the herd. They have zero fear. They even allow the shepard to mentor them. They only select partners that support protection and growth and stability of the herd. If you ever watch a sheep dog, you will notice their actions are precise and simple and seem rather boring. If you were to ask a sheep dog why, their answer would be "because I am a sheep dog, and I always do the right thing for the sheep."

The difference between a wolf and a sheep dog is that the sheep dog professes the "moral high ground." I have spent my life among sheep dogs and wolves. They are the same. An outsider would never be able to notice the difference. I like the wolf because they adapt the best of all character types. If you were to ever meet a wolf and ask them why they are doing what they are doing, the only answer you will ever get is "because I said I would do it." They don't justify, explain, or even care if you agree or disagree. To a wolf, any explanation regarding "why" is relegated to sheep.

The wolf wastes nothing. No actions are ever wasted during the day or at night. They communicate in a short precise manner facts and thoughts. The cliché of action is born from the wolf: "Never stand when you can sit. Never sit when you can lie down." Each wolf is very strong and mentally even stronger: they are all built and self-trained to endure. A wolf never risks injury unless to protect the pack or family; they often walk away from situations where injury is likely. The immediate pack are their only partners. But they will welcome another into the pack only when that new member proves capable and committed.

They have laser-precision focus, using every one of the five senses. Wolves are emotionally stable within the pack and rarely display residual emotional issues because every member in the pack will both listen empathically and also punish quickly emotional responses. Every wolf embraces failure and fear and continues to confront and learn from failures. A pack of wolves will push each other constantly to improve. The pack dynamic is built on mentorship: demonstrate, be patient, yet demand outcomes. The single goal of a wolf in a pack is to grow the pack and keep the pack safe. It is that simple and that big at the same time. Because a wolf knows it is a wolf.

Finding the Den

In training clients, I made no distinction to select one of the character assessments over another. My assumption regarded wolves to be the ones drawn to the intense training and methodical approach, yet I was completely wrong. The training drew all four types in equal numbers. I too was very surprised at the soliciting of the omega character trait. To date, not one omega or fringe person has been able to complete the training for the simple fact they cannot overcome their reasons or excuses. The fundamental truth of a measurable, outcome-based life is that excuses will always dominate actions: a clearly brutal existence. Watching the drama unfold and also draw me in was intolerable, and each has been dropped from training for inability to do three simple things.

The sheep or follower trait shows up frequently. The sheep trait literally self-imposes three major issues, each rather difficult to overcome. Sheep play too small. I find it very hard to play with people whose goal is to get by or get along or maintain status quo. The second issue reflects a part of the soul that further makes working with someone extremely difficult to produce results. Drama and emotional weakness are so difficult to negotiate with. But I have learned patience and my own personal willpower to push them toward their results, which aids in outcomes. The third self-imposed weakness of the sheep trait that delays success is their unwillingness to select partners who push them. I have yet to fully understand what inside of a person with a sheep trait prevents them from having partners who are better and smarter than they, not to mention their utter refusal to do what the professional partner suggests they do to grow.

The sheep dog trait is the most abundant in clients. Sheep dogs always are trying to improve themselves and always looking to help the sheep they guard. They make promises and keep them without fail: always enthusiastic, always on time, and always completing every assignment exactly as directed. They are warm, generous, welcoming, and very family oriented. The life of a sheep dog is quite extraordinary, and they grow and learn systematically and never fall apart.

Now, the wolf is not easy to train nor easy to find to train. Once found, the wolf says, "Prove to me first." The wolf is inherently skeptical and impatient with new ideas and new people. The wolf is already very aware of "who they are" and are already playing a game that is extremely difficult to win, and they know it. The wolf already has laser focus, already has the emotional stability required to thrive in difficult times, and already pushes their limits and have zero fear.

For three years in retirement I sought to find a den of wolves and my approach was wrong each time. The sheep needed help and leadership in each of the sections of the formula. The sheep dog needed clarity on "who they were," because service required them to not support themselves and family as much as they do the herd. And the sheep dog required new partners and new plans because when they were only living in the "bubble" of the herd, they got stale. Offering the training to the wolf using the same approach as the sheep and sheep dog missed the mark every time.

The wolf did not want to be approached or sold anything. They are a complete paradox in business because I could not sell them anything. They wouldn't even take something for free; they would not take bait off a hook. If they didn't earn it themselves, they would not take anything, ever. So I stopped hunting for the den of wolves entirely.

After three years of living my life, protecting my family, growing my business, running in ultramarathons, making mistakes and asking for help, and never making the same mistake twice, a wolf approached me. Let me say that differently so that I make my point clearer. The wolf is always watching for weakness or strength. The wolf abhors weakness, because weakness means death. The wolf is drawn to strength because strength means life and growth. That is the fundamental truth of the wolf.

Bring Home Meat or Don't Come Home

Joe is a wolf. Very straightforward in communication and intent. Not mean, not full of himself, just on point. When we met, I noticed no fear, which usually is the case when someone meets me who had never met a SEAL. And I hate that part of society who fear SEALs and think we are so different that we are treated either worse or better than others.

He just said, "I want you to show me what you learned in your life as a SEAL and how you are still applying it in retirement."

"Well, I don't show people anything unless there is a deep commitment to grow as a person," I said, not trying to hurt his feelings. Stacy often corrects me for my curtness with people when I am not in the mood.

He sat there and didn't change expression. "I read your book and you like being uncomfortable and have recovered from loss many times. If that is true, show me how you do it. I want to learn a new way to be uncomfortable."

"What are you committed to achieving, and who are you doing it for?" I asked because those answers would tell the story, and if he couldn't answer each, I could go back to what I was doing.

"My top leaders are having a training, and I want you to show us all what you have learned so that we have new skills," he said, still sitting there without changing expression.

"Joe, my training is uncomfortable and exposes weaknesses and often can make people cry and be frustrated. Are you sure you want to see that in your crew?" I asked, pushing back.

"How much time do you need to show us one thing that will make us better leaders or better people?" he asked.

I recall thinking how odd to be sitting there across from a wolf who wanted what he wanted and patiently awaited the answer. Most people take so much subtle convincing and coddling to take a bold step. "I need eight hours to demonstrate two aspects of leading during chaos," I stated. As I began to discuss the details, he stopped me short.

"If you can demonstrate those two and we walk away with those two skills, I will pay you whatever you charge. If you cannot, then I won't pay you a single dollar. Those are my terms," he said without threat or emotion as he stood up. "My partner will contact you for details. Can you be prepared in five days from now? If not, I will find someone else."

"Joe, I can do tomorrow if your crew is ready. You have to participate, or the training will have no value to your crew or you as the leader. Those are my terms," I said, chuckling as we shook hands and he accepted.

"I would not ask my team to do anything I was not willing to do myself. We look forward to spending the day with you," he said, and with that, he was off.

That night I recall discussing with Stacy the offer from Joe and the terms. As with most protective and strong women, she was skeptical. "Thom, no one does business on a handshake anymore for that amount of money, especially in a consulting arrangement. You should have gotten half up front," she scoffed.

Let me share a truth regarding the state of mind I had at the time, one that I had spent years pitching and discussing and convincing prospects of the merit and upside to the process and method of three simple things . . . I was tired. I was tired of directing the sheep to having purpose and ownership of their own lives. I was tired of overcoming the excuses that come from people unwilling to do three simple things a day, even if it meant success and millions in the bank. This was an opportunity to grasp the excitement to play a game again where the reward was only on the back end. No reward for showing up, no money for the attempt, just bring home meat or don't come home mentality was more exciting than the comfort of getting paid up front.

The remainder of my time was spent rehearsing the topics and demonstrations for a group setting and being critiqued by Stacy. The process of rehearsing is uncomfortable for me, and that is the reason for it. Even in the SEAL teams, rehearsals were an assault on the ego and exposed weaknesses. In this instance, Stacy could not understand the demonstration, which caused a fight and moments of tension. After the fourth attempt, I could see the "light bulb" of understanding turn on for her and she smiled and said, "Okay, that was amazing. Question is, will you be able to do that again?"

Honor

The event proceeded without incident and concluded with payment. As promised, the seminar exposed points of weakness and solutions to overcome each. Many opportunities to be uncomfortable and vulnerable arose, and Joe was the first one to confront each as the leader. The details of the process and methods I used to expose the weaknesses and even the solutions have little value outside the context of Joe's team. The important point to pass on is the level of discomfort required to achieve success.

After decades of being around wolves and top organizations, the first point of success and growth comes from the level of discomfort the boss is willing to take into his or her life. The boss cannot defer the discomfort or pain to another. The boss cannot go to a safe space and fumble until perfection. Great leaders are always willing to stumble in front of the people they lead. Joe stumbled like a pro. And, like a pro, he asked to do it again and again until he figured it out. Then he watched patiently as each of his team stumbled again and again until the result was achieved. He was not condescending or angry or put off.

After 23 years of working with and for wolves in the SEAL teams, I enjoyed the lack of drama while working with Joe and his crew. Just simple engagements with no excuses and no drama was amazing to watch as a trainer. They all were committed before showing up to the event instead of the normal conflict of waiting to see the result before committing to the process.

Each person, including Joe, practiced and stumbled on integrating the three simple things we had selected that would benefit the team.

Each leader then saw the benefit of the simplicity of the activity within the grander scale of complexity the organization had found itself in. But it was very uncomfortable to watch and very uncomfortable for each to experience iterative failures.

The environment around a wolf is set up to live this life: the life of uncomfortable existence. Change is always uncomfortable and risky. Emotionally, change causes resentment for the discomfort; frustration, because the new practice is hard or different to do; and many either get sad and upset or angry when they cannot figure it out the first time. Yet this uncomfortable life works through change rather quickly every time change is initiated.

The wolf honors the life of discomfort and change and is patient with process and methodologies that enable solutions. I call the environment around the wolf one of honor and respect for the people who embrace the uncomfortable life of change. Joe's leaders display honor much like the SEAL teams. They all make promises and keep them. They all embrace failure and discomfort as a means to solve complex problems and make them simple. Each doesn't react emotionally when mistakes happen. And, most importantly, each is committed to process and methodology and displays rock hard patience until the end. To be quite honest, I did not think this environment existed outside of the SEAL teams. Maybe I had given up on finding the wolf den?

Relentless Hustle and Follow-up

Over the next several months, Joe and I would meet once or twice a month to talk simply about things in our lives that mattered most. We agreed to no business pitches, no drama, no uncommitted discussions, and no nonsense. Any topic could be thrown out on the table if the topic mattered.

The whole dynamic of what I call "eating meat with a wolf" reminded me of the straightforward interactions with SEALs who I had shared combat experiences with. Short sentences with no fluffy words. Laughter on topics others would think serious or nasty. Most striking is the feeling of peace. SEALs are at peace with themselves around other SEALs. Wolves are at peace in the company of other wolves, because everyone gets to eat what is on the table.

As with all things I do, I filter all of my interactions through the formula and where the new points would possibly fit into my five formulas. I often try to determine how the people I am interacting with have properly or improperly "filled in" their formula and the impact of the usage. In short order, Joe knew who he was quite clearly and could articulate his five goals. He also could articulate his companies short, medium, and long-term goals.

Joe centered his entire business model around finding and training the best people and compensating them for "bringing meat to the table." What they sold as a product or what service they provided did not factor into how Joe looked at his people and his business. Centering everything around people as the thing you lead got my attention for the simple fact SEALs centered every aspect of the organization around training the people and ensuring the people had access to whatever they needed.

And Joe never asked why. The question of "Why?" never came up in a single conversation we had for six months. Once we were talking about a situation in his life that I would have expected him to question himself. I asked, "Joe, do any of your leaders ever question you, what you are doing or why you are asking them to do something?

"Only weakhearted or unsupported people ask why. I stopped asking myself why because I never found an answer that was convincing enough," he said, laughing. Then he got serious. "You must be going through something if you are asking the why question so subtly."

"No, Joe, I stopped asking the why question during Hell Week for the same reason. Any answer to why is nonsense. I do things because I said I would do them. That is the only answer powerful enough to overcome any obstacle to make me ask why," I said laughing, watching his expression change to a smile.

Every conversation we had for months centered around the people equation. Or, rather, how to get the best version of the person he hired out into the open. He shared the three traits he looks for: hungry, resilient, and holistic. The first character trait had to be demonstrated from the first encounter and held up throughout every meeting. Each person literally had to show Joe they would hustle in everything they did. I laughed as he described his straightforward process and noted, "Well, that weeds out half the pool, doesn't it?" He merely smiled, saying, "Without hunger as a genetic code, being around me will kill them; so yes, it weeds out those who are not, very quickly."

Joe went on to explain resiliency, "we want proof each new person has failed once or twice before we put them through our training. We know the training will be too much at first for each person, and if they have not bounced back before, they will resist being coached to try again. Sales is really all about bouncing back from failure or hearing no."

Finally, the trait of holistic is so vague, I had to pin down Joe with a description of how that is tested and evaluated. I expected a long discussion centered around moral high ground and doing the right thing for the right reasons. But I was completely surprised when he merely said, "Each of us has to take care of every aspect of our lives and be willing to have others on the team to challenge us when we are not taking care of each aspect."

In my mind I said "bingo" quite loudly, and for a moment I looked at Joe because I thought I had said the word out loud. "Wait, you mean HR doesn't prevent you from suggesting everyone eat well and works out? And you allow your team to talk to you about personal issues?" I asked. "I have worked with many organizations that talk a big game, but HR prevents a great deal of those types of interactions with employees. Do you allow yelling and fights and crying?" I asked.

"No fighting in the office or public space, but yes, fighting doesn't get you fired when there is so much tension, it may be needed. I am okay with it if I don't get blindsided by the event. To be straight, I make them all sign agreements with me that they will meet the detailed demands," he commented as if the question was a moot point.

"Joe, do you mind if I watch and see for myself a day in the life of Joe and team?" I asked, inviting myself without thinking the invite would hurt his feelings.

"I was going to invite you to one of our meetings, because I wanted you to poke holes in what we do. You don't seem to care much for how people could be hurt from pointing out a mistake. And I want to see if you can add value. When you come and sit at our team table, then you have to add value and not just observe. We do things in real time and solve things in real time. Feel free to point out anything that you could improve. Just be careful, the team is wicked smart," he said, and I accepted.

The meeting was not what I have witnessed in 80 percent of the businesses. No one came to socialize. Instead, each of the direct reports came to gain insight and keep the momentum going on the project they were assigned. And Joe wasn't in charge of the meeting; his head of operations clearly was in charge and quite capable. Minus the kill orders and assault assets of the SEAL teams, the meeting progressed with the precision and competence I missed.

1. Three-minute dialogue of who we are, what we do, and the outcome desired upon conclusion of the meeting

2. Two-minute review of some important follow-ups from last meeting and how were resolved and what remained unresolved and a report back, date and time

3. Seven-minute around the table on key topics and key projects and decisions that had to be made right now

4. Five-minute dialogue from Joe to each direct report, helping solve the point that was raised

5. Two-minute discussion from Joe regarding next future initiatives and ideas that will be coming soon and what to expect in the next three weeks

6. Five-minute discussion regarding what is going on in the background that is or could be impacting each member's work and life

7. One-minute review of due outs from the chief of operations

Twenty-five minutes of lethal meaningful discussions, and out the door they all went except for the chief and Joe. The pace slowed down as I watched the two discuss the team. The 25 minutes reflected the format of problem/solution/recommendation/and follow-up. The after meeting clearly looked like two SEALs right after a mission talking about the intangible issues that each had experienced.

Joe asked, "How is the team handling the increased pace and responsibilities?"

"We had to send two managers out to Detroit to convey the direction changes and what the sales team had to do to adjust. That was something we all hadn't discussed. Change always impacts preexisting plans with their families," the chief remarked.

"Oh, I did notice the sales follow-up application reflected several calls at 2 a.m. with sales reps. How is the manager and sales rep dealing with the long hours?" Joe asked patiently with pen in hand waiting to take notes.

Their discussion was very private about the people and the impact of the life on each of the direct reports and what she recommended Joe do immediately to follow up with two of the staff. As I watched the exchange, it struck me as odd that the two would share so intimately in front of me. "Joe, do you want me to leave? This seems private," I asked, not wanting to infringe.

Joe said, "No, I am sure this is the same stuff that happens in the teams; hiding or running from it just increases the distance to the solution. And I want to hear what you have to say about each person and the meeting."

Once the chief left, Joe and I sat for a moment until it was quiet once again.

"What did I miss?" he asked.

"Interesting meeting," I said. "I only took two notes the entire time, which is strange for me because I tend to find problems in everything, and I hate that of myself," I said while opening up my book. "My first note is why is Joe here? I wrote that down because for several minutes, that answer was unclear. The second note is because I personally want to know the answer. What is the financial upside to your being here and making those decisions?"

"Never thought about that. I don't know if I can track a decision and the revenue generated, because I made the decision. Do you know how to track that?" he asked.

"I ask because I am trying to pin down the value of a CEO's time. The value isn't what they are getting paid relative to hours spent at work. Watching you all conduct a leader's meeting much like we did in the SEAL teams, the thought occurred to find out the measurable impact of the time a CEO spends addressing a problem through another's action versus solving the problem himself," I said, gingerly relaying my thoughts.

"When did the problem occur and what was the immediate loss of time and revenue? Then, when was the decision from the boss given and a solution provided? Those may be distinctly different issues. Then, when was the issue actually solved and the upside realized? Might be fun to figure that out. I am going to figure it out anyway with your company or the next one I consult with," I declared.

"Wait, I want to know that now too. Delays are costly; they never are good for business in any way. Okay, solve it. Take whatever time you need, and you have full reign to solve that problem," he said, tasking me.

Come Back Carrying Your Shield or on Your Shield

The differences between the omega, the sheep, the sheep dog, and the wolf are both subtle and also "crystal clear." The subtle difference is the similarity in how each uses language to fill out the formula of human performance. Each does know exactly who they are, which is the first line item of the formula. However, the omega, the outlier, fills out the declaration statement with who they are not. The sheep knows he or she is a sheep, as does the sheep dog and the wolf.

The omega and the sheep do not actively fill in their individual goals; instead, they allow each day or predicament to define what they will accomplish and when they will accomplish it and where. Meanwhile, the sheep dog and wolf will dictate their goals by sheer force of will. The vast differences in the two groups clearly separates each from the other.

Line item three does separate each of the four clearly and may be the key differences that later lead to success or abject failure. The omega literally has no need statements, no drive to change, and no initiative whatsoever. Maybe other people smarter than me have solved the riddle of the omega type, but I have not been able to impact the lack of focus, the emotional void, and the unwillingness to fail. And without clarity there, the omega type of human is stuck on the proverbial "X." The sheep focus on immediacy. Whatever the day brings or is in front of them, they focus on . . . without having the ability to change focus. The sheep are very emotionally reactive to every sound or impulse as if the world is ending. And the sheep fears failure and will never openly fail for any reason. A sheep lives in the self-imposed limits the world has constructed.

The sheep dog, however, focuses solely on protecting the herd. I call this skill external focus. All their senses are attuned to each in the herd and all the external threats. A very useful skill to acquire in life, to be sure. Yet the sheep dog neglects focusing on itself. The paradox is alarming when you witness the sheep dog trait. It's emotionally very stable when it comes to dealing with the herd and protecting the sheep from outside threats. However, when left alone, the sheep dog becomes emotionally fractured and can quickly become ill and, in despair, convert into an omega type. Most special operations soldiers associate with the sheep dog and have a similar emotional composition. Regarding failure and pushing limits, the sheep dog will constantly go above and beyond any limit the environment places on the herd or the sheep dog. He will jump off a cliff to protect the herd. She may confront a pack of 20 predators without hesitation. Highly focused, emotionally stable unless left alone, and completely without fear, knowing no limits.

The wolf has the highest capacity to focus and to be intentional. Unlike the sheep dog, the wolf does not always stay on point 24 hours a day. I call the way the wolf trait uses focus is much like the "Hulk" from the cartoons. One moment the wolf is calm and playful, and the next the wolf has exploded into the terrible killing machine. A split second later, the wolf can convert back into a playful mom or dad. Emotionally, the wolf trait has the widest range of emotions of all the traits, and you can witness hundreds in a day: love, hate, rage, happiness, frustration, calm, regret, tenderness. While hunting, a wolf will only use an emotion that helps the hunt. While leading, a wolf will demonstrate a wide range of emotions, from dominance to patience, with the pack. The wolves' entire hormonal system is uniquely tied to emotions, and these emotions are often completely under the control of the wolf. The wolf always pushes each situation to the extreme. The wolf knows no other way and playfully tests limits for fun. Yet the travesty of the wolf trait is fear. The wolf has no fear of dying. The wolf fears injury because injury would cause the wolf to lose respect of the pack and to possibly be kicked out of the pack. This point may be a surprise to you as you read about the wolf trait, but fear is a deep emotion for every wolf I have ever met. Fear of not being allowed to be a wolf, fear of rejection from the pack.

My interactions with Joe reminded me of the wolf trait. He had surrounded himself with direct reports and a sales force who were a mix of sheep dogs and wolves. The most interesting aspect in his business was he had no sheep traits. I had expected some sheep because, sadly, most businesses are filled with sheep that just stay in their collective boxes and do work within the box. The twist of the team structure was that the sheep dogs kept the wolves safe and in control, and the wolves were free and encouraged to hunt.

As I watched and often interviewed various people within the organization, I witnessed an environment much like the SEAL teams. The environment is openly constructed around the wolf being free to hunt and operate as a wolf. Let me further explain that. The business wasn't operating on a timecard, no hourly employees, no siloed people sectioned off from the group. Everyone was on the team, or in the pack, to aid in getting the wolf to hunt. The wolf was required to hunt, not manage the pack.

Take a moment and imagine the power of a team operating together with the sole intent to hunt and bring home meat and share that meat with the pack. The unique aspect Joe had put in place for the wolf, or salesperson, remains the most brilliant aspect: sharing with the pack. Imagine working on a team knowing you played a vital role in the winning and in the losing. Imagine knowing if you made a mistake, you wouldn't get as much pay, yet if you overachieved, you would get paid more.

"Joe," I said, knocking on the door to his office to inquire into this team arrangement, "I notice everyone here actually knows what they are doing and who they are doing it for. Let me ask you a question. What is the most important trait you are looking for to be displayed by your entire team?"

He looked up and said, "That is a simple answer . . . loyalty to one another. Self-serving people, even if they are the best salesperson or best at a particular position, destroy the team environment. I have fired many of the best salespeople because of the lack of loyalty. No backstabbing here, Thom. I demand each be responsible to his or her actions and the impact the actions have on the team. And we have to account for each other's actions in public. I demand that if someone is hurting or needs help that other people help them, whether that help is in their unique job specification or not. If you ask for help here and the help isn't given, that person is gone. We are project oriented, so we don't concern ourselves with time at work. I find project focus causes the conditions for loyalty and helpfulness."

Their culture comprised of: loyalty to the team, wolf and sheep dog traits, constant training through demonstration and follow-up, and project orientation, all designed around people. The organization structure lends itself well to measuring the impact of the best use of the boss's time. The first key factor in the boss' time was, paradoxically, how much time he spent at work engaged with meetings and employees. The more time Joe was at work engaged in meetings, social discussions, or interviews with staff or future employees, the less time the company had to engage in work. The less time they actually hunted for meat. In contrast, the more Joe was out recruiting new business and pursuing future opportunities, the more lethal the salesforce and management team was.

The second key aspect of the boss' time had to do with demonstrating how to live life to the company. Take a moment and attempt to understand that whatever a boss demonstrates, so do the employees mimic. Joe took time to demonstrate his commitment to his personal health by both being fit and eating well and changing clothes and walking out and going to work out. This simple act and use of time literally increased the health of each employee. One hour of the boss working out has a compound effect on the success of each employee because they too will take time and work out. He would also have his kids come to work and show them respect and demonstrate family. One hour of seeing the boss with his family caused the 30 staff members to spend quality time with their families.

Joe and I discussed this measurable advantage of leading the pack by living openly in front of the pack. During the discussion he asked how he could better demonstrate his commitment to each of his employee's "life."

"Joe, I can tell you the best way to demonstrate your commitment to your staff is to do something incredibly difficult with them outside of the grind of work. I train leaders by taking a group of leaders out each quarter to demonstrate leadership skills by doing a 24-hour event. I know of no quicker and easier method to show them how to lead and live and be a part of their struggle. The sad fact of the matter of leadership is that you have to confront chaos and lead during chaos. Anyone can parse off difficult situations and suggest what to do in the event of a crisis. But leading during chaos is a muscle that requires constant development," I said, pausing to determine if he was willing to take on the challenge.

"So let me get this correctly: you are suggesting both me and my direct reports do your 24-hour event collectively?" he asked me rather skeptically.

"More than that," I said. "Your wife is a part of the executive team and she has to play too." I grimaced as I suggested this key point because a wolf is very protective of family. "In 24 hours, you will be exposed personally and as a team to the real chaos that surrounds each of you. Nothing can stay hidden for 24 hours! I want to warn you what will come up and may happen. You will want to quit; your wife will want to quit; and perhaps many on your team will want to quit. What will happen to your team if one or any of you quit?" I asked.

"We won't quit," he said.

"Joe, stop the BS. What will your team do if you quit?" I pushed back.

"Interesting notion. Well, if one of my team quits, I would probably lose respect and eventually get rid of them," he answered rather quickly.

"But what if *you* quit?" I stood my ground.

"Probably the same would happen," he eventually answered.

"Right, so are you willing to lead during chaos? Because chaos is not something to control, and you have a great deal of control here in the office. Can you control the simple things you will be going through for 24 hours and aid others to control the simple things under their control and not blow up and quit?" I laughed as I asked it.

Prior to Joe's crew participating in the 24-hour challenge, I had already held 10 separate events. Each event saw at least four people quit. No matter what I did to change the event, I could not prevent quitting. Walking for 24 hours seems simple but becomes rather complex in the final 6 hours. Pain seems real, and most people quit when pain is a real factor. Nausea and exhaustion, too, become justifiable reasons to quit. The hardest obstacle, however, for each person to overcome is the sense of isolation that descends. Most cannot deal with the feeling of isolation that happens when darkness falls and pain gets worse and exhaustion sets in and everyone around is annoying in every way possible. The unconquered mind and soft soul lose focus on taking simple steps and become very committed to finding an exit ramp.

As we gathered prior to stepping off and never stopping for 24 hours, Joe stood up and said, "You all will either come back with your shield or we will carry you on your shield. We will all complete this event, no matter what."

I was shocked. Trust me, I am rarely shocked. I did not want to cause a business to fall apart and lives be disturbed because Joe would fire the quitters. Stacy and I discussed how "the word on the street" regarding the 24-hour challenge would change from a leaders' training event to a brutal "last man standing" event if a company were to show up and people got fired. I reluctantly stepped off, thinking this would be the last one.

After the first four hours, Joe came up and said, "You were right, I want to quit. All of a sudden, I don't want to be here, and I cannot get it out of my mind."

"You know why, because this is the real you showing up, and it is disturbing, isn't it?" I pointed out.

The next 6 hours, I could tell, isolated Joe. He was not used to what he was experiencing about himself. The group as a whole had difficulty staying together at whatever pace I walked. For me the pace had not changed from walking at three miles an hour which meant each person was in the darkness of their own thoughts and issues. On hour 14, Joe's wife turned her ankle. Normally, with most groups, a turned ankle would always make that person quit, and other people would follow.

As Joe approached, my mind flashed back to all the SEAL students who would approach me when I was instructor. I had realized, then, that no motivation or encouragement from me would change their mind. My friendship with Joe was five steps away from dissolving into excuses and rancor. With that, I turned my brain off and prepared for the vomiting of excuses I was so sure would follow.

"She turned her ankle really bad. It is swollen," he said.

"Joe, this is your life. Either quit and excuse yourself, or stay and let's figure it out," I said, trying not to sound cold. "I can tell you this injury is a self-imposed limit. You both can stop, and this will forever be a limit. Or you can explore what else is available if you don't quit. Seeking my guidance won't solve your limit, it will just validate it. What if a hurt ankle isn't the issue here?"

"I don't want her to be injured permanently," he stated.

"Joe, injuries to the body are not permanent. They are all a façade or scar tissue. The real damage comes from inside. You know this, but you don't allow your family to feel pain. That is the wolf inside you, by the way," I said, pausing to see what he would do.

"Let's play it out, then. I will stay back with her and help. We won't be able to stay with the group, though," he suggested.

"Well, if you stay, I bet the group will stay with you. That is the reality of not quitting. Leading during chaos happens now. Most leaders don't ask for help, so chaos reigns. If you ask for help, things get really simple, really quickly," I instructed.

At the 24-hour mark, everyone remained. I had learned to allow the real conversations to come to the surface every time we stopped instead of disregarding them. I had learned to deal with the real chaos people encounter each event by talking about it and allowing for real dialogue about each experience. Each pain, each level of exhaustion, and each darkness people experienced was the "tip of the iceberg" of the deeper thoughts they were having. Not talking openly about each was the chaos. Talking about them in gory detail caused simplicity.

The 24 hours was actually physically and emotionally harder than the others had been, at least for me. More hills, more miles, helping the injured was harder in every way. But everyone made it through.

Every one since then has been progressively much harder. And the harder each becomes physically, coupled with the deeper the conversations become, conversely make more people get through. Now we have had to limit the number of people at each event, because a huge group becomes isolated and chaotic once again.

"Joe, I have determined the measurable value of your time," I said, as I grabbed his hand to shake it at the end.

"Well, I feel less now, so I am interested only slightly," he said, chuckling.

"Your value of the time you spend with the key people is in the actual lives and outcomes they have each day," I said. "As short or as long as is required to see them produce results. I don't have an equation for that, and I don't think I want to pin that down."

The Method: Know the traits of your team and reinforce the need for constant improvement. Lead during chaos by immersing yourself into it to solve for simple actions. Never give up on yourself or your people.

Be Bold: The Comfort of Discomfort

Success is simple, but not easy. I've worked with people just like you. People with busy lives, multiple responsibilities, businesspeople, and athletes. My training is hard. You must be willing to live with the discomfort that will inevitably be part of the commitment to three simple things in each of the five pyramids. Are you sick of making your life complicated? Are you ready to commit to six hours of baseline activities each and every day? No matter what kind of chaos life throws at you? Are you willing to endure discomfort for 21 days? The three simple things are simple. They require to honor your word and never give up. We are ready. Are you?

* * * * *

A Personal Note from Joe Caldwell

"When we met, my team and I had already built a thriving business, but as we're always looking to challenge the status quo and push ourselves to newer/higher limits, we decided to bring Thom to speak to our top producers and teach them his framework of simple actions to drive better results. Everyone walked away with a clear definable plan and the simple actions to achieve the directive. The storms I've had to face personally, and in business since meeting Thom, would have appeared insurmountable in the past. Chaos would have ruled and reigned. Doing the very simple things repetitively have been the stones that are paving a path of gold in my life and business. More than the results I've seen in my life and business, the friendship we've developed over many a coffee, meal, or shooting guns is one that I will cherish forever. He is the real deal, full of heart and wisdom."

—Joseph Caldwell, CEO, Consolidated Assurance LLC